W9-AGH-958

How Money Walks

How $2 Trillion Moved Between the States, and Why It Matters

HOW MONEY WALKS

How $2 Trillion Moved Between the States, and Why It Matters

By Travis H. Brown

Copyright © 2013 Travis H. Brown, all rights reserved.

How Money Walks

How $2 Trillion Moved Between the States, and Why It Matters

By Travis H. Brown

Copyright © 2013 by Travis H. Brown

All rights reserved. No part of this book may be reproduced in any form or by any electronic or mechanical means, including information storage or retrieval systems, without permission in writing from the publisher, except by a reviewer, who may quote brief passages in review.

Published by:

Travis H. Brown
Pelopidas, LLC
1034 S. Brentwood Blvd.
Suite 1700
St. Louis, MO 63117
www.pelopidas.com

For speaking engagements, press inquiries, and media appearances, please contact the author:

Travis H. Brown
travis@howmoneywalks.com
(314) 435-4527

For more information on How Money Walks, *please visit:*

www.howmoneywalks.com, or scan here:

PRINTED IN THE UNITED STATES OF AMERICA BY WORZALLA, STEVENS POINT, WI

THIRD EDITION, JANUARY 2014

ISBN: 978-0-9887401-0-5

CONTENTS

CONTENTS

ACKNOWLEDGEMENTS

This book would not have been possible without the privilege of working directly for those passionate about keeping our American Dream alive. Through the last seven-plus years that my wife Rachel and I have worked with philanthropists, such as Rex and Jeanne Sinquefield, it has become increasingly clear that all citizens should have access to how income is moving within America. The migration data referenced in this book provides essential insights into an important factor in how and why Americans are moving within our country. All U.S. citizens should have a clear understanding of how our country, our states, and our communities are doing economically.

That's where the quest to find this data started. Thanks to the previous cooperation between the United States Census Bureau and the Internal Revenue Service, all taxpayers can learn from one another in meaningful ways over the long run. It is our hope that Congress will help keep this most basic information available to the public in the future.

As is so often the case, the raw data itself was less meaningful until it could be made more user-friendly via comparisons and contrasts. Completing this task would not have been possible without several key people who are part of the Pelopidas team. I need to thank Lucas Tomicki for his brilliant efforts interpreting and mapping the IRS data; Larry Stendebach for his technical assistance with the Web site, app, and all things digital; Stephanie Abbajay and Brooke Foster for their editorial assistance; and Emily Iles for the design and layout of the book.

Along the way, it seemed clear to us that we had to explain how and why this data might seem surprising or hard to comprehend. We would like to thank the numerous organizations that have provided further insights, such as the Tax Foundation, the American Legislative Exchange Council, Laffer & Associates, and the National Taxpayers' Union.

I am deeply appreciative of the many great writers and thinkers who added personal perspectives to the goals of this effort, including: Art Laffer, Joseph Calhoun, Deroy Murdock, John Tamny, Thomas Del Beccaro, Niger Innis, Rex Sinquefield, and Victor Sperandeo. Such a diverse cross section of experienced leaders may not have come together without the help of Laura Slay, Alexandra Preate, and Dan Holland.

Lastly, a special thanks goes to my family: to my wife Rachel, for her tireless support in every section of our lives; to my father Harold, for inspiring the work ethic that "can't never could;" and to my mother Louise, who proved the value of going the extra mile through her own creative productions.

Foreword

IT'S ABOUT TIME

By Dr. Arthur Laffer

When I read *How Money Walks*, I thought, "It's about time." Finally, we have a book that addresses one of our nation's most critical (yet rarely discussed) fiscal issues: the migration of working wealth as a direct result of personal income tax rates. Travis H. Brown's book, elegantly presented and based on data rather than rhetoric, paints a clear portrait of where money goes and why.

As an economist, an investor, and an advisor, I have spent much of my professional life thinking about tax structures. Again and again, I return to this essential question: how much taxation is too much, and what kind of tax impedes economic growth? Through decades of research and real-world experience, I have found that the personal income tax is one of the least productive forms of taxation.

Brown's *How Money Walks* should serve as a wake-up call for states imposing punishingly high tax rates on their citizens. Income is a highly mobile asset. As this book shows, between 1995 and 2010 over $2 trillion moved from high income tax states to states with lower (or no) income taxes. Small businesses and working families vote with their feet. They bring new wealth—not to mention new jobs and new ideas—to states with more benign tax structures.

These concepts are no mere academic exercise to me. In fact, my personal experience is reflected in this book. Many years ago, I chose to leave California (which currently has the nation's highest top marginal personal income tax rate and the fourth highest per capita state tax burden) and relocate my business and my home to Nashville, Tennessee. Nashville is a lovely city, to be sure, but it's Tennessee's pro-growth tax environment—the state levies no income tax on salaries—that drew me here and will keep me here. As Brown shows in this book, hundreds of thousands of Americans are making similar decisions.

There are many things I appreciate about *How Money Walks*. Chief among them is Brown's dedication to data-driven research. This work is objective, not subjective. By using 15 years' worth of IRS-provided taxpayer data, Brown makes arguments that are ironclad. Tax migration is not a partisan issue, nor should it be used as one. I've spent my career advocating for fiscally sound tax policies that are best for all working Americans. I served as economic advisor to President Ronald Reagan. I voted for President Bill Clinton. My support for both leaders had much to do with their pro-growth, responsible fiscal policies and less to do with partisan politics.

For decades I have championed the idea (most famously with the Laffer Curve) that we can actually expand government revenue by cutting taxes, and that growth can be encouraged by simply lowering or eliminating personal income taxes. The proof, as they say, is in the pudding, and we see the evidence year after year: the states with benign tax policies are the ones that are growing while the states with high taxes are the ones that are declining. The American Legislative Exchange Council's yearly comprehensive study of the 50 states and the District of Columbia, *Rich States, Poor States* (of which I am one of three authors, along with Stephen Moore and Jonathan Williams), documents this, and I am pleased that Brown is able to use our findings here as well. The numbers don't lie.

How Money Walks should be on the bookshelf or e-reader of every American concerned about the wealth disparity among our states. It should be required reading for anyone who wants to understand why some states struggle to retain people and businesses while others welcome billions of new dollars each year. This book is straightforward, fascinating, and important.

Dr. Arthur Laffer is the former chief economist at the Office of Management and Budget and a former economic advisor to President Ronald Reagan. He is the founder and chairman of Laffer Associates and Laffer Investments and the co-author of Rich States, Poor States, *published annually by the American Legislative Exchange Council.*

Introduction

MONEY WALKS BECAUSE OPPORTUNITY TALKS

The interesting thing about movements is that you don't always realize one is taking place until after the fact.

Of course, there are exceptions. In the early fall you can look up and see Canadian geese heading south and understand that they are migrating for the winter. And certain historical population shifts were visible as they happened: think of the nearly 40,000 Irish who landed in New York City in 1847 during Ireland's potato famine or the 200,000 people—both Americans and foreigners—who moved west in the 1840s and 1850s during America's great western expansion and the California Gold Rush.

But most movements go largely unnoticed until someone sees compelling evidence of a sizable shift, usually over a long period of time. That is what is happening today. Another great movement is taking place right now. It is a movement of millions of Americans with over *$2 trillion* in adjustable gross income (AGI). And it's happening right under our noses.

According to the Internal Revenue Service, from 1995 to 2010 over $2 trillion and millions of Americans moved between the states, leaving some states with deep net losses in both population and AGI, while some states saw amazing gains in both categories. Though many economists and reporters have been following this trend and have even written about it (Art Laffer, Stephen Moore, Jon Bruner at Forbes.com, economists at the Tax Foundation, and others), few Americans know about it. It is not usually part of our national dialogue.

Until now.

How Money Walks explores this great movement and—using definitive data mapping of IRS taxpayer records—shows exactly what is happening in this country, where the incomes started and where they moved. For some states and metropolitan areas, it's a pretty picture. For others, it's a nightmare of loss.

What is driving this massive movement? Well, we cannot be 100 percent certain of the cause, but, as you will see, the data points to a very clear, very compelling correlation: over the long term, money moved to states where taxes were lower. But not just any taxes—personal income taxes.

Between 1995 and 2010, the period for which IRS taxpayer data files are available and the period I examine in this book, the states with high personal income taxes saw enormous losses, while states with low or no personal income taxes enjoyed massive gains. In total, Americans moved $2 trillion of their adjusted gross incomes in and out of the states between 1995 and 2010. Two trillion dollars is about the annual GDP of California, the ninth largest in the world. It's *a lot* of money. And when that much income moves between the states, it warrants a little scrutiny, don't you think?

~

I'm a political consultant and legislative lobbyist by trade. I am the president of Let Voters Decide, a voting advocacy organization, and the co-founder of Pelopidas, LLC, a political consulting firm, both in St. Louis. I have an MBA, an undergraduate degree in agricultural economics, and am a contributor to Forbes.com, but I am not an economist. So why my interest in this subject? Why write a book about it? Because I am an entrepreneur. I am a businessman, and I understand growth and incentive and the importance of incomes. I also understand that taxes are important not just to states and governments, but to people as well. And there is no tax that arguably has more impact than the income tax.

Income tax has been the subject of debate and analysis since the Sixteenth Amendment—ratified on Feb. 3, 1913, some 100 years ago—codified a national, uniformly applied income tax. The national income tax has served as a model for the various states' own personal income tax structures, for better or worse. Nine states impose no state personal income tax, while 41 others, plus the District of Columbia, impose income taxes of varying degrees.

Economists and analysts have spent decades researching the effects of income taxes, both federal and state, and it is still as hotly debated as ever, even more so today given the state of the U.S. economy, the national debt, and the country's finances (remember the fiscal cliff?). Though the intent of the income tax is clear—the government levies taxes (in this case on personal income) to collect revenue to provide services—experts and pundits differ on its effect. Does it hurt consumer spending (the basis of 70 percent of our nation's gross domestic product)? Does it weaken the economy? Is it the best source of revenue? Is it fair?

Lots of questions, with lots of different answers and opinions. But we know this much: first, when you tax something you get less of it. Second, when you tax personal income, you take away a person's *control* of their income, which reduces the level of economic choice they have. This also has an emotional impact. People don't like to have their incomes taken away; they prefer to *choose* how they are taxed. For example, you have control over how much property tax or consumption tax you pay based on your behavior—you can choose where to live and what to buy and pay the attendant tax based on that choice. But when it comes to taxing income, you have little choice.

Unless, of course, you choose to move and take your income with you. You pay federal income taxes no matter where you live, but state personal income taxes vary widely, and I think millions of Americans took advantage of this between 1995 and 2010. As we shall see from the data in the following chapters, $2 trillion in adjusted gross income moved from high-tax states to states with low or no incomes taxes. Money walked, I believe, because the opportunity for people to keep more of their incomes talked.

Income fuels most of our personal decisions in life. Generally speaking, your income dictates where you live and how you live. The size of your house, what you spend on clothes, where you eat, what you buy, the car you drive, where your kids go to school—all of these life choices are made based largely on your personal income. Incomes matter.

But not only does income fuel your personal economy, it fuels the nation's economy as well. Everything flows from personal income, be it consumer spending, investments, or taxes. And the more income people have, the healthier the economy. That's why the income tax is so important. Whether you think it is a necessary evil or a burden that should be abolished, income tax reduces the amount of money people have to save, spend, or invest, potentially putting the brakes on economic growth and development.

I care deeply about American growth and prosperity. I want this country and every one of its cities and states to grow and prosper. And when I see massive income migration and economic growth in some places and stagnation and deterioration in others—when I see *trillions of dollars* of aggregate incomes fleeing some states and moving to others—I have to ask, why is this happening, and why aren't we talking about it?

~

If you are losing your working wealth to other states, you are losing your most precious cargo. These are your earners, your workers, your entrepreneurs; this is your tax base. This great movement of working wealth into and out of states is staggering and has serious economic ramifications. I think it is imperative for all Americans—you, me, politicians, planners, economists, soccer moms, hockey dads, *everyone*—to pay attention to it and, possibly, figure out why some states and cities are growing, prospering, and attracting people and incomes while others aren't.

The national federal income tax turns 100 on February 3, 2013. The income tax is deeply rooted in this country, and there is much rigidity in our nation's tax policy. Yes, there have been tweaks and adjustments through the decades, but the nation's income tax has survived virtually intact for 100 years. That's a very long time for anything to survive, let alone a program that is loathed by so many.

This anniversary presents us with the opportunity to start a national dialogue about income taxes. It is, to many people, inconceivable that the country, let alone most states, would do away with something so firmly embedded and ostensibly so necessary as the income tax. But the playing field isn't exactly a level one. Yes, everyone (at least those who qualify) pays federal income taxes, but there are nine states with no state personal income tax. As we shall see in the ensuing chapters, those nine states are the ones that enjoyed the biggest boom in the migration of American working wealth, in this case calculated by AGI.

And the robust presence of AGI—real working wealth—is a great indicator of economic vitality. Did people take their money and move where state income taxes were low or nonexistent? Does money walk because opportunity, in the form of no or low income taxes, talks? We shall see.

~

In the heated and partisan debates over taxes and economic policy, I believe that it is possible to offer a view that is neither partisan nor inflammatory. *How Money Walks* offers a dispassionate examination—using official IRS files of real reported aggregate incomes from real Americans—that shows where the working wealth of this nation went and where it came from. My intent is not to take sides with any political party or school of thought, but to educate people about where working wealth has gone in this country and, maybe, encourage all Americans to take a harder look at the reasons behind the movement.

This book explores the massive movement of America's working wealth, how money walked, where it started, and where it went. The whys are subject to debate but the facts are not. *How Money Walks* shows where the income went—and where it started—as reported to the Internal Revenue Service by the taxpayers themselves.

Personally, after spending several years mapping and analyzing this data, one correlation keeps popping up: income moves to where it is most welcome, tax-wise. Money walks because opportunity talks.

See for yourself. And then let's get the conversation started.

~

Note: At the end of each chapter, you will find a QR code; simply scan the code with your smartphone and you will be directed to a site that has supplemental and additional material, illustrations, video, and other information. QR code-reader apps are free and are widely available for download. Visit our Web site, www.howmoneywalks.com, for links.

Chapter One

THE $2 TRILLION BOMBSHELL

Working wealth walked, and we know where

Imagine, if you will, that over the last 15 years you received, just by being you, a windfall of over $86.4 billion. Yes, *billion* dollars. Every year, for 15 years, an average of $5.76 billion arrived on your doorstep, and you didn't have to lift a finger.

Congratulations. You are the state of Florida.

From 1995 to 2010, according to data from the Internal Revenue Service, the state of Florida saw $86.4 billion in actual taxpayer-reported adjusted gross income move into the state. Not projected income, but real, adjusted gross income (AGI) as reported by tax-paying Americans on their federal 1040s.[1]

What is AGI? It's all the income that Americans report on their federal 1040s from all sources, including wages and salaries, business income, interest and dividends, capital gains, rents, royalties, alimony, annuity income, inheritances, pensions, etc. I call it working wealth.

It's hard to fathom how much $86 billion is. No one has ever held that much money in his hands. But here's a comparison: according to Forbes, $86.4 billion is roughly the market value of Starbucks, Taco Bell, Pizza Hut, Kentucky Fried Chicken, Dunkin Donuts, Papa John's, and Chipotle. *Combined.*[2]

Still too big to imagine? Let's break it down. Florida saw a net gain of $86.4 billion in AGI over 15 years. That's $5.76 billion a year, $15.7 million a day, or $10,958 every minute that came into the state of Florida from 1995 to 2010.

That's some big money. Imagine how proud any policymaker would be to have added even a fraction of this AGI to their state. That would be some achievement.

But here's the kicker: that income *moved* to Florida from other states. This wasn't natural-growth income from Florida residents—in other words, income reported from new or existing jobs by people who live in Florida. Rather, this was income that *moved* into the state of Florida from other states. People—almost a million over the course of those 15 years—simply moved to Florida and brought their incomes with them. Florida's gain was some other state's loss.

How did Florida do it? What caused this great migration of income? Maybe it was the sunshine. Maybe it was Disney. Maybe it was the beaches. Maybe it was the fact that Florida has no state personal income tax and a relatively low state tax burden per capita. Maybe it was a combination of all those factors. It's hard to tell, and there is most likely no single factor that caused the movement. But we do know this: from 1995 to 2010, almost one million taxpayers moved into the state of Florida, bringing with them $86.4 billion in reported aggregate income.

How do we know this? From an unimpeachable source: the IRS. My associates and I have mapped the migration of aggregate income in this country using a cache of IRS data from federal 1040 forms from 1995 through 2010 (the last year for which this information is available, as of this printing). This data shows that an extraordinary and unprecedented movement took place of approximately *$2 trillion* in aggregate income across the country. And no one seems to be paying any attention to it. Until now.

That's the purpose of this book, to draw attention to this great movement of working wealth and to try to understand some of the reasons behind it. And with recent federal efforts to discontinue public access to this data, sharing this knowledge may become an important call to action for all future journalists, economists, and citizen taxpayers alike.

~

First, let's be clear on what we are talking about. When you file your federal taxes, you calculate your adjusted gross income. AGI includes all sources of income, both active and passive, such as:

- Wages and salaries
- Business income
- Interest and dividends
- Capital gains
- Rent, royalties, and alimony
- Pensions, life insurance, and annuity income
- Inheritances

AGI—or aggregate income, as it is also called—represents income *before* taxes. I refer to it as working wealth because it is what people earn; it's their total income, and it represents the strongest indicator of a person's wealth before taxes.

Again, we took the most recent taxpayer data files available from the IRS, 1995-2010. This 15-year period offers a broad view that favors no single president, administration, congress, or state- or local-level representation. This is income information from the most official source: the IRS. It reflects an expansive view of the American economy and offers a big picture overview rather than a single snapshot of income migration. And when we step back, we can see a clear pattern of movement: money moved from high-tax states to low-tax states.

We went broad, but we also went deep. From that IRS data (which was massive, by the way), my associates and I created a year-by-year, state-by-state, county-by-county database and mapped it for ease of use. Every county in the country in every state is represented, and we can see exactly how each county and state fared in every year from 1995 to 2010.

We also mapped the data by metropolitan statistical area, or MSA. MSAs are geographical collectives defined by the Office of Management and Budget as the country's metropolitan areas. MSAs are the entities that most people recognize as "cities." Unless you live in a rural area, most people identify themselves as living in a city. And even if you don't live in a city proper, you probably identify yourself as living there anyway.

For example, say you are on a flight to Los Angeles and your seatmate asks you where you live. If you live in Webster Groves, Missouri, you say you live in St. Louis. If you live in Florissant, Missouri, you also say St. Louis. If you live in Glen Echo, Maryland, you say you live in Washington, DC. If you live in Arlington, Virginia, you also say you live in DC. People generally have an economic, geographic, and an emotional attachment to an area.

The reason we looked at MSAs is that they are large but specific economic and geographic groupings that provide a much more accurate reflection of how an area is doing than merely looking at a city proper. A city—strictly speaking—is too narrow. An MSA, on the other hand, is a more accurate reflection of an economic region. For example, you may live in the city of St. Louis (as I do) with a population of 318,000, but the St. Louis MSA actually consists of a much, much bigger geographic, economic, and population area, one that encompasses millions of people (2.8 million, according to the Census Bureau) and thousands of square miles.

I have taken all of this data from the IRS and the Census Bureau and mapped it to track the migration of working wealth in this country from 1995 to 2010. And I've created a Web site, www.howmoneywalks.com, that anyone can access, along with an app that enables readers to localize the data and see how their own state, MSA, or county is doing. The app is called *How Money Walks* and you can download it by scanning this QR code:

Once you have the app, simply enter your zip code and you can find out how your area fared over those years. The findings may surprise you.

From this database and map, we can see where America's working wealth came from and where it went. No matter where you live, if you are an American citizen with an income over a certain amount, you must file a federal 1040 return and report your adjusted gross income.

More to the point for our purposes, filers also have to indicate where they live. If a filer moves from one year to the next, the filer reports that, the IRS takes note, and we see it in the data. For example, if a 1040 filer moved from New York to Miami in a given year, the data shows when that move happened and how much aggregate income went with it. If a 1040 filer moved from Chicago to Seattle, same thing.

We can see where the incomes started and where they went, and when we map it out over that 15-year period, a clear migratory pattern emerges. Money, and a lot of it, is walking all over the country. We know where; the question is, why?

Let's return to Florida to start looking for answers. From 1995 to 2010, $86.4 billion in adjusted gross income moved into the state of Florida. The biggest source of moving wealth? From our database, we can see that it came from New York and New Jersey. Collectively, those two states sent $27 billion in AGI down to Florida over those 15 years, $16.8 billion from New York and $10.2 billion from New Jersey. That's $27 billion in working wealth that didn't stay in New York or New Jersey. That comes to $1.8 billion a year ($5 million a day), which is just about what the New York Metropolitan Transit Authority netted in 2011 from tolls on its bridges and tunnels.[3]

And here's the thing about that income: it stayed in Florida. It's not like New York or New Jersey lost it one year but it migrated back. No, it moved to Florida and it stayed there. Lost for good in most cases. Good for Florida and bad—*very* bad—for New York and New Jersey.

But other states contributed to Florida's net gain: over the same period, Illinois lost $6.1 billion in AGI to the Sunshine State, Ohio lost $5.9 billion, and Pennsylvania lost $5.6 billion.

Though Florida gained the most of the $2 trillion in AGI that migrated from 1995 to 2010, it is not alone in its big gains. Other states also enjoyed massive influxes from the migration of aggregate income.

According to the IRS data, from 1995 to 2010:

- Arizona gained $24.5 billion, mostly from California and Illinois
- Texas gained $22.1 billion, mostly from California and Louisiana
- North Carolina gained $21.6 billion, mostly from New York and New Jersey
- Rounding out the top five is Nevada, which gained $16 billion, more than half from California alone

Those are the big winners. Of course, if there are big winners, there have to be big losers, too. After all, this is a zero-sum game: the money moved, leaving one state and going to another, so if some states gained billions, others lost billions. Florida, Arizona, Texas, North Carolina, and Nevada are the five states that saw the greatest net gains in AGI. The five states that lost the most aggregate income over the same period? They are:

- New York, which lost $58.6 billion
- California, which lost $31.8 billion
- Illinois, which lost $26.1 billion
- New Jersey, which lost $18.5 billion
- Ohio, which lost $17.1 billion

These are staggering sums, and it's hard to really fathom what the figures mean. To give it some context, just those five states alone lost $152.1 billion in aggregate income from 1995 to 2010. According to Forbes, that's roughly the market value of Ford, GM, and Volkswagen combined.[4]

Let's take a quick look at the biggest loser, New York. Between 1995 and 2010, $58.6 billion in aggregate income left New York State.

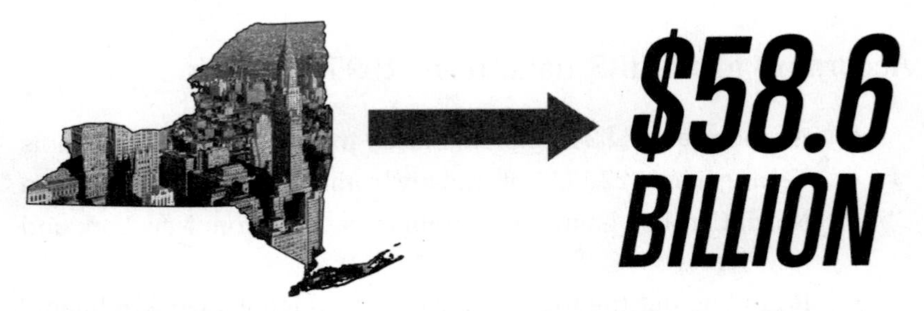

That is roughly enough money to fund the 2013 fiscal year state budgets of North Dakota, South Dakota, Montana, Wyoming, Idaho, Oregon, Kansas, Nebraska, Mississippi, Arkansas, and Iowa combined.[5]

How on earth did this happen? Why is aggregate income fleeing some states and flocking to others? Again, many factors come into play. People move for all sorts of reasons—jobs, family, school, weather, taxes, etc. It is difficult to draw clear conclusions or determine exactly why people move. However, when you look at the mapped data over this period of time an unmistakable pattern emerges: income moved from high-tax states to states with no state personal income taxes or lower per capita taxes.

Clearly, many factors play a role in income migration patterns. Money walks for many reasons. I am not drawing a causation about migration and taxes (although you might after reading this book and seeing the data), but there is an undeniable correlation here. The proof is in the pudding, as demonstrated by the mapping of the migration of aggregate income in this country. From that, we can draw a clear correlation to the idea that taxes matter, and that incomes migrate to where state income and other taxes are low.

Income is our most mobile resource. We can see that in the data. People have been moving by the millions with trillions of dollars. We know that. And we also see one common factor: people seem to be moving where they can keep more of their personal income.

This brings us to a word about methodology. As stated, the data used in the mapping and which will be used throughout this book was taken from federal taxpayer 1040 files, as compiled by the Internal Revenue Service and made publicly available by the Statistics of Income Division (see endnote number one). Statistical and geographical definitions and population figures are from the Census Bureau.

There are limitations to the IRS data:

- The data is from 1995 to 2010, the last year for which IRS data is available and consented for release. This is a 15-year period, as the data goes to 2010, but not through 2010.
- There is a difference between tax year and migration year. Since tax returns are filed in the year following the tax year, the migration year is almost always the year following the tax year. For example: a taxpayer files his 1997 return in April of 1998 in Michigan. He then moves to Illinois and files his 1998 return in April of 1999 in the state of Illinois. The IRS data in this case would show a migration occurring between 1998 and 1999 from Michigan to Illinois, while the AGI for this migrating tax filer would be his 1997 tax year.
- The data reflects all taxpayers who file in a given year up until late September of that year. By IRS estimates, this represents 95-98 percent of all taxpayers. While the data reflects almost all tax filers it systematically underrepresents some groups of Americans, specifically those who are not required to file a tax return (usually the very poor and the elderly). In addition, it does not include the few percent of taxpayers who file after the late September deadline. These are generally very wealthy taxpayers who have been granted extensions by the IRS. As a result the migration data underrepresents the very poor and the very rich.
- The data also excludes tax filers who change filing status between migration years. For example, if a married couple files jointly in

a given year, then moves and files separately the following year, the data would reflect only one tax filer moving.

- Data reflects tax filers, not individuals. For example, a single tax filer may represent a family of four if a married couple with two children is filing jointly.
- For a tax filer to be classified as having moved, he needs to have moved between counties. Moves within a given county are not counted as migration.
- Since the address used for filing one's taxes does not have to be one's primary residential address, certain types of situations may create an impression of migration when in fact the residential address of the taxpayer has not changed. Examples include:
    - A tax filer with multiple residences who used one filing address in one year and changed to a different address the following year;
    - Students who might file using their parents' home address in one year but file from their university address the following year;
    - A tax filer who decides to use his business address for filing purposes, while he used his home address in previous years;
    - A tax filer who uses the address of the tax preparer or financial institution for filing purposes and previously used his home address;
    - A tax filer who uses a post office box address and previously used his home address.
- The data reflects adjusted gross income. AGI includes all sources of income, both active and passive, such as (but not limited to) wages and salaries; business income; interest and dividends;

capital gains; rent, royalties, and alimony; pensions, life insurance, and annuity income; and inheritances.

- At the county-to-county migration level, there must be at least 10 tax filers moving in a given year for the migration data to be included in the IRS files. This is done to prevent individual taxpayers from being potentially identifiable should there be only a small number of movers. In the case of some tax filers being omitted from the county-to-county migration data, they would still be included in the state-to-state migration data. As a result, the sum of all county-to-county migration may not add up to the state migration totals in some cases.[6]

We combined the taxpayer data from the IRS with data from the Census Bureau to build a geo-database that could be easily mapped and analyzed. This wasn't terribly complicated, but it was time consuming and required fairly sophisticated technology. It wasn't easy, but it can certainly be done by anyone with the technology, know-how, and interest.

Why that time period, 1995 to 2010? Because that's what the IRS made available. We didn't choose that period specifically; it's simply what the IRS made available and consented for release. But this time span offers a good and broad picture of the economy and of the migration pattern. We'd like to go back many more years but taxpayer data files are not available before 1995 in a format that is easy to analyze.

And why did we track personal income? Many reasons. First, as I've previously said, personal income is the most mobile of resources, and it is a data point we can actually track using official information from the IRS. People take their income with them, and, from the IRS data files, we know where it started and where it went.

Second, adjusted gross income represents the most comprehensive definition of income used by the IRS, and includes all sources of income, making it the least biased measure that can be analyzed.

Most important, AGI is not biased by state and local taxes because it represents income before taxes. Nor is it biased by the taxpayers' individual situations because it is a measure of income before adjustments, exemptions, and deductions, which are driven by the individual's filing status and number of dependents.

Since AGI is the broadest measure of income, it is a good proxy to personal income, and personal income is important because every facet of the economy stems from personal income.

PERSONAL INCOME			
spending	saving	investments	taxes

There can be no taxes without personal income. There can be no consumer spending without personal income. There can be no savings or investments without it. There can be no growth without it. Income is the basis for all things.

That is why we focus on AGI. It is the most important barometer of economic health and is a leading indicator of how economies and governments can operate. It's like your pulse: if your pulse is strong, your body is strong. If your pulse is weak, your body is weak. Same for the economy: if income growth is strong, the economy is strong. If income growth is weak, the economy is weak. Pretty simple.

That's why AGI matters and that's why we mapped it. It's unbiased, it's easy to track, and it's a reflection of economic conditions. If people are moving into your state and bringing their personal incomes with them, that is a strong indication of growth. If people are leaving your state and taking their incomes with them, that is an indication of weakness. Mobility speaks volumes. As entrepreneur Paul Kedrosky wrote on Jon Bruner's *Forbes* blog:

> Economic vibrancy is about mobility. It is about where people come from, and where they go. It is about where they were, and where they want to be—about needs and aspirations. The porosity of borders to human talent's movement facilitates ingenuity-sparking collisions to our benefit.[7]

In other words, when people move, bringing their smarts and their incomes with them to their destination, there is growth. And why do they move? Again, all sorts of reasons, but clearly opportunity and incentive are compelling, which we will explore in the next chapter. The other thing about income is that it is emotional. Income is what you've earned through employment and hard work or through investments or other activity. It's yours, and you make life choices based on your income. Income doesn't guarantee happiness but it does guarantee choices.

~

For the purposes of this book, we are not going to look at every state, county, or MSA in the country. That's overwhelming, though all of that information is available on the Web site. Instead, we are going to offer a general overview of the 10 states that gained and lost the most AGI and then drill down to the 10 metropolitan statistical areas that gained and lost the most AGI.

Why metropolitan areas? Again, it's because America is driven by its cities. It is where the vast majority of Americans work and live. It's where the most commerce takes place ("gains of trade," as taught in economics in college). You can really see the results of tax and economic policies at a local level. By looking at the MSAs we get a clearer picture of income migration and, perhaps, a clearer understanding of why income moves the way it does.

Two trillion dollars is a lot of money. It's California's GDP, the ninth largest in the world.[8] Why didn't anyone notice this much wealth moving around? Well, lots of reasons.

First, it happened over time. It is hard to notice a trend or a migration pattern when it happens over a 15-year period. It's not as obvious as if 100 ships pulled into a harbor and disgorged thousands of people all at once, or if there was a massive caravan heading west. It's not like you woke up one morning and every family on your street had packed up and left during the night. This was gradual. It didn't happen overnight. Despite the enormity of the movement, it largely went unnoticed. It was not—again, despite the vast amount of money involved—a high-profile event.

Second, it wasn't announced. No one put a sign in his yard saying, "I am moving to Texas because there is no income tax there."

This is a subject people don't usually talk about and it is rarely covered in the media. You never hear news stories about money moving because taxes are lower somewhere else. You also may not know anyone who moved because of taxes. It is off our radar screen. The migration was not televised. It was not high profile, so our brains simply didn't register it. You may have noticed a massive change in a place like Detroit, where thousands of homes and office buildings stand empty and thousands of people left for other places. And you may have noticed it in boomtowns like Austin and Phoenix, both of which nearly doubled in size over this period of time.

But in vibrant, popular places like Miami, New York, Los Angeles, or Chicago, which hustle and bustle 24/7 with people constantly coming and going and businesses constantly opening and closing, you simply don't notice migration. There are just too many other things going on all the time.

Third, when the data becomes available, it is often misinterpreted. Income migration is often attributed to factors like the real estate market (both boom and bust) and retirement, but the important thing about this movement pattern, as evidenced by the IRS data, is that this is working wealth; these are incomes not based solely on retirement and investments. Also, because it happened over a 15-year period it cannot be chalked up to so simple a factor as retirement or real estate.

So no one was looking for it. We simply didn't notice it because we were paying attention to other things. That's the fourth reason: our brain simply doesn't work in a way that notices this sort of movement. The brain registers two different things very well: high-profile events that occur infrequently, like plane crashes, or low-profile events that occur with high frequency and high degrees of flexibility (and over which you have control and an active choice), like getting gas. I bet you know exactly how much you paid for gas yesterday, and I am willing to bet that plane crashes register deeply with everyone, though they are infrequent and rare. Your brain, for various reasons, tells you that these things are important, so you pay attention to them.

In the case of the plane crash, even though the probability that you'd be involved in or affected by one is miniscule, your intuitive brain tells you to pay attention. In the case of gas prices, if you drive a lot, getting gas is a high-frequency event and one in which there is usually a great deal of choice between stations A and B, so your brain tells you to pay attention, and you register that information. But the movement of income is different; it's low profile and a matter of private record. Incomes are generally a private matter. If you didn't participate in the movement, it didn't register with you.

Fifth, income taxes fall under the category of rational ignorance. Sounds scientific, but it's actually very simple. Rational ignorance means avoiding something that you feel is inherently negative, or avoiding an action that you feel you cannot likely or easily change. We don't notice the things we don't want to see or feel we cannot change. And that is exactly what happens with income taxes.

When it comes to income taxes, most people feel they have no choice or flexibility. For the vast majority of people, income taxes are something they never even feel; the money is taken from them before they even get it. It is abstract, and they feel they have no control over it and no choice in the matter. Therefore, the brain says, "This is not something you need to pay attention to. But did you see the price of gas and hear about that plane crash?!"

Most people don't want to talk about income taxes. Though widely loathed (does anyone enjoy paying them?), income taxes are also widely accepted as a fact of life, something we can neither control nor change. So we are rationally ignorant of them and, accordingly, rationally ignorant of any movement that may be the result of them. Most people don't even know how much they paid in income taxes last year. People feel they have no choice, and therefore they do not focus on it.

But there is a great deal of choice when it comes to paying personal income taxes at the state level. Yes, you have to pay federal taxes, but, depending on where you live, your state personal income tax could be zero or it could be more than 13 percent. Big difference.

People move for real reasons, not just the weather, and, although we may not know what those reasons are, the movement is not random or arbitrary. People leave a place for a specific reason and they go somewhere else for a specific reason. It's not random, and maybe we just don't want to see it.

~

So, why does this matter? Why should you care if people are moving? Why should you care about the migration of aggregate income? Why should you care about personal income taxes? Why should you care if your state has low taxes or high taxes? Because the presence of aggregate income, of real working wealth, is the single biggest contributor to and barometer of the health of your local, state, and national economy. This is not esoteric. This is how growth is measured.

The robust presence of aggregate income—the kind people may or may not pay taxes on (depending on how much they make and where they live) but most assuredly spend—is the single biggest driver of the U.S. economy. Why? Because 70 percent of America's GDP—the measurement of the country's total economic output, including production, spending, and everything else—is based on consumer spending. Our economy runs on it. The more money people have to spend, the better our economy does. The converse is also true: the less we have to spend, the poorer the economy fares.

That is why personal income taxes matter. No other tax is as important to the well-being of the American economy. Jim Clifton explains it perfectly in *The Coming Jobs War*:

> America needs to simultaneously cut taxes and raise business output so there are a lot of jobs and everyone has money to spend at the mall, to fix up their home, to buy fishing equipment. A massive 70 percent of U.S. GDP is based on consumer spending. So when consumers' take-home pay is reduced, by default, they lower their spending and subsequently lower the GDP.[9]

This is true locally, regionally, and nationally. Our economy cannot grow if people do not spend money. It's that simple.

Furthermore, it bears pointing out the obvious: there is one and only one source for taxation–income. Yes, you may derive your income from investments or gifts or whatnot, but everything started in the same place, with income. Without income there is nothing–no taxes, no spending, no investments, nothing. With income there is growth. With income people can spend and invest. And where there is income, governments can tax and provide services.

Why should you care? Because the more people there are to pay taxes, the less you should have to pay. If you live in an area where lots of working wealth has left, that means the pie has shrunk, and the tax burden falls more heavily on those who remain. If you live in an area to which AGI has migrated, the burden shrinks.

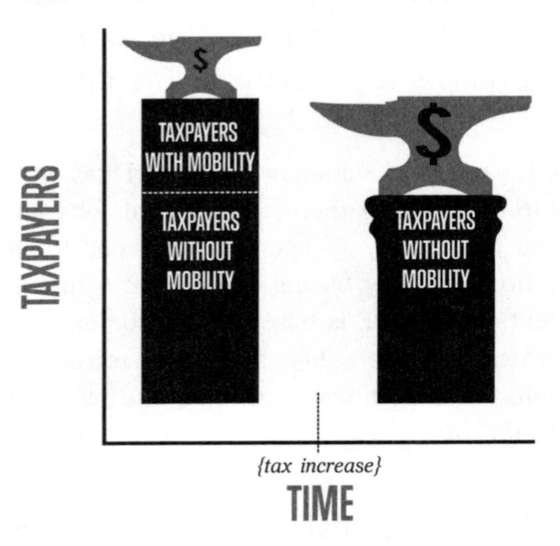

If you doubt this, just look at California. Based on the IRS data, we know that more than 300,000 people left between 1995 and 2010, and the state saw a net loss of $31.8 billion in AGI. And California's taxes continue to go up (the voters there just approved another tax increase this past November, making the top marginal tax rate 13.3 percent, the highest in the country), so the burden falls more and more heavily on those who remain.

But it's not just taxes; it's the vibrancy and health of the local economy, too. Where there is lots of AGI there is positive economic activity—growth, jobs, spending, etc. There is increased opportunity. Where there is a loss of AGI there is the opposite—fewer jobs, fewer businesses, less commerce, less opportunity. It's pretty straightforward:

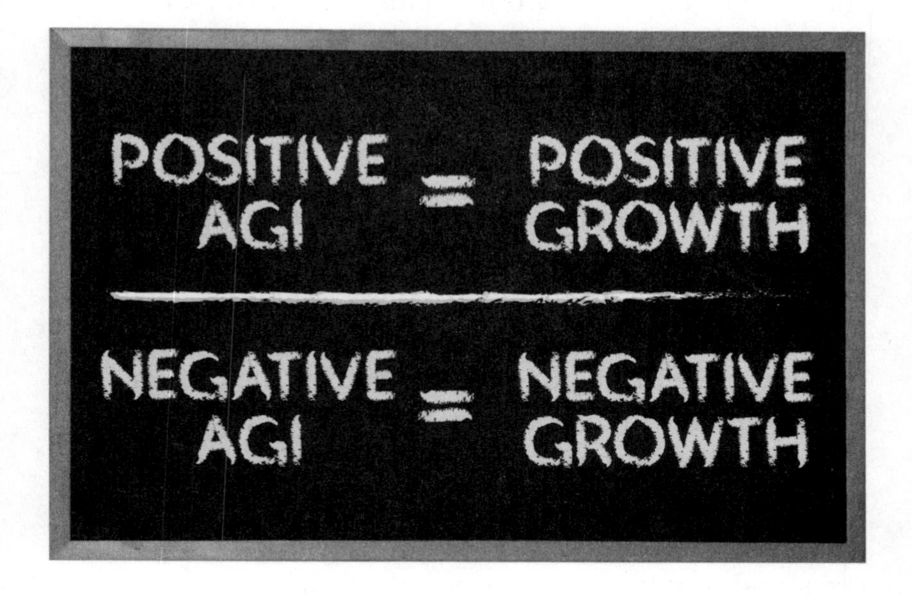

You may not care about the big picture issue of income migration, but you certainly care about the pulse of your community or state, and we measure that by the presence of AGI. Where there is robust growth in AGI, the area grows. Just look at the Las Vegas MSA, where Zappos is investing $350 million downtown. Where AGI leaves, things start to fall apart. Again, look at California, which continues to lose people and working wealth (mostly to—yes—Nevada) and continues to raise taxes to support those who stay. The presence of AGI has a direct benefit or cost to you. You should care a great deal.

From the IRS data we can see that some states and MSAs are attracting huge sums of AGI, while others are losing tens of billions of dollars. And we can also see that the states and MSAs that are attracting the most AGI are the ones that are growing (like Las Vegas), and the ones that are losing AGI are the ones that are faring poorly (Detroit). This will be covered in depth in ensuing chapters.

That's why it is imperative to look at the numbers and try to understand why income is fleeing certain areas and why it is moving en masse to others. State per capita tax burdens vary widely and those may or may not play a definitive role in migration. The key may not be any one factor, but the movement is undeniable: wealth, in the form of adjusted gross income, appears to be migrating from states with high personal income taxes and high per capita taxes to areas with low or no personal income taxes and low to moderate per capita taxes.

The amount of money people are able to spend is the single biggest contributor to the economy, both locally and nationally. And people cannot spend money if their taxes are too high. This is why taxes, most especially personal income taxes, matter so much and have such a profound effect on the American economy: the more income you get to keep—and the more you get to make decisions about how to spend your money—the better.

Since everyone has to pay federal income taxes (if you qualify, of course), a major way for people to keep more of their income is to move to states where the personal income tax rates are low or nonexistent. That's what I think this great movement is all about. People are moving out of high-tax states and into states with low or no personal income taxes, so they get to keep more of their income and have a greater say in how they spend it. They are voting with their feet. I think money walks because opportunity, in the form of keeping more income, talks.

~

You may not be interested in what your local, state, or even federal government is doing regarding tax policies. You may not even care about taxes in general. But you certainly know income when you see it, and you certainly understand what it is like to have it and have more or less of it depending on your personal income tax rate.

And you certainly understand the benefits that accrue when a city or region enjoys an accumulation of wealth through income migration—growth and development—and when the opposite happens—stagnation or, worse, deterioration.

As a leader in any community, you might be better off measuring AGI rather than population, because AGI shows real economic activity, real people, and real growth. Population only shows a number.

You don't have to be an economist to appreciate the pattern of income migration that is apparent in the data mapping. It's happening, and it appears that there is a direct correlation between state personal income tax rates and income migration. Money is walking, and we can see exactly where it's going.

Clearly, this analysis is retroactive; we are looking at IRS data from 1995 to 2010. But it is my belief that past performance *is* an indicator of future behavior. I believe money will continue to walk to where it is most welcome.

~

The purpose of this book is to educate, so that if you are a politician you can make better choices and better decisions, and if you are a citizen, you can be better informed and perhaps encourage your representatives to make the choices that lead to real growth for your region, state, and country as a whole.

This is not a political book. This is not a policy book. This is not an academic book, though it is based on official statistics and data. This book won't give policy prescriptions or calls to arms or offer platform planks for political parties. What this book simply does is draw your attention, with unimpeachable evidence from the IRS and Census Bureau, to the very real facts of where this nation's taxable income started and where it went. Working wealth is out there, and it is mobile. And we know how important it is to the economic health of any city or state. So, here is the key question: is your area attracting working wealth or driving it away?

America does not sustain losers for very long. Losers either change for the better or they stagnate and die. So, what do the numbers say? They say that a startling amount of income is moving, every year, into and out of states and MSAs. Where is the income going and where is it coming from? Is your state or region welcoming working wealth or driving it away? See for yourself.

Scan here for supplemental and additional material, illustrations, video, and other information. QR code-reader apps are free, and are widely available for download for all handheld devices. Visit our Web site, www.howmoneywalks.com, for links.

Chapter One Endnotes:

[1] All adjusted gross income and population figures are taken from IRS data, 1995 to 2010. In this context, 1995 to 2010 is a 15-year period, as the IRS statistics go *to* 2010, but not *through* 2010. Internal Revenue Service, Statistics of Income Division RAS:S, P.O. Box 2608, Washington, DC 20013-2608.

[2] Market values as of October 2012, Forbes.com.

[3] Jennifer Fermino, "Toll revenues up though traffic on bridges and tunnels down," *New York Post* (February 27, 2012), http://www.nypost.com/p/news/local/toll_revenues_up_though_traffic_PnueHA97ZjRpGJntRR5N3L.

[4] Market values as of October 2012, Forbes.com.

[5] State FY2013 budget figures from Sunshinereview.org.

[6] For more information please see "U.S. Population Migration Data: Strengths and Limitations" by Emily Gross, IRS Statistics of Income Division, http://www.irs.gov/uac/SOI-Tax-Stats---Migration-Data-Users-Guide.

[7] Paul Kedrosky, "Migration in America: Vibrant Flux," Data Driven blog, Forbes.com (Nov. 16, 2011), http://www.forbes.com/sites/jonbruner/2011/11/16/migration-in-america-vibrant-flux/.

[8] California 2011 GDP and world economic ranking, http://www.ccsce.com/PDF/Numbers-Sept-2012-CA-Economy-Rankings-2011.pdf.

[9] Jim Clifton, *The Coming Jobs War* (New York: Gallup Press, 2011), p. 32.

Chapter Two

MONEY, MOBILITY, AND OPPORTUNITY

Why money moves, and why it matters

Before we dive in and look at which states and MSAs gained or lost working wealth, let's talk briefly about wealth and opportunity and explore in greater depth the ideas of why money moved and why we didn't notice.

First, why do people move? Lots of reasons: jobs, family, school, sunshine, etc. Sometimes people move because they have to make a major adjustment for personal or professional reasons. Sometimes people don't really get to choose. But very often, people move for opportunity. Clearly, no one is going to uproot and go through the hassle of moving if a better opportunity wasn't waiting at the other end. They are willing to take the risk because of a perceived reward. People don't just move. It's not random. They move for real reasons, and that often entails opportunity and incentive.

There's sociological and economic theory behind that idea, too. It's called the Theory of Intervening Opportunities and it was conceived back in the 1940s by Harvard sociologist Samuel Stouffer. His theory states: "The number of persons going a given distance is directly proportional to the number of opportunities at that distance and inversely proportional to the number of intervening opportunities."[1]

In other words people move because there is a better opportunity somewhere else. That's what smart people do—they make choices based on opportunities, and one of the greatest and most important choices a person can make is where to live. All things being equal, would you rather live in an area with a strong economy or a weak one? Would you choose an area with many opportunities or few? Would you choose to live in a state with a high income tax or no income tax?

I realize that last question is simplistic, but the 15 years of data we mapped shows a clear pattern of AGI—real money, working wealth—moving from states with high personal income taxes to states with no or low personal income taxes. Those states happened to experience tremendous growth over the same period. Did money walk because opportunity and incentive talked? And did that opportunity come in the form of low taxes?

Yale law professor Michael Graetz, a former deputy assistant secretary for tax policy at the Treasury Department, has written extensively about this trend. In his book *100 Million Unnecessary Returns,* Graetz articulates a clear connection between high income taxes and migration:

> When corporate and individual income tax rates on capital income are high, that income tends to move to a jurisdiction with lower rates. Often the capital—and its accompanying jobs—moves. Sometimes only the revenue is lost through tax planning. In today's highly competitive global economy, high income tax rates are counterproductive.[2]

What we see in the data is telling. There are nine states with no personal income taxes. Let's compare income migration figures for the nine states with no income taxes with the nine states that have the highest personal income taxes.

The nine states with *zero* state personal income tax:

STATE	NET GAIN (OR LOSS)
Alaska	($1.4 billion)
Florida	$86.4 billion
New Hampshire	$3.2 billion
Nevada	$16 billion
South Dakota	$528 million
Tennessee	$8.3 billion
Texas	$22 billion
Washington	$9.9 billion
Wyoming	$1.3 billion
	Total gain: $146.2 billion

The nine states with the *highest* marginal personal income tax rates:

RANK	STATE	NET GAIN (OR LOSS)
1	California (13.3%)	($31.8 billion)
2	Hawaii (11%)	$198 million
3	Oregon (9.9%)	$5.6 billion
4	Iowa (8.98%)	($3.2 billion)
5	New Jersey (8.97%)	($18.5 billion)
6	Vermont (8.95%)	$693 million
7	Washington, DC (8.9%)	($3.4 billion)
8	New York (8.82%)	($58.6 billion)
9	Maine (8.5%)	$1.6 billion
		Total loss: $107.4 billion

The states with no income taxes gained over $146 billion, equivalent to about three and a half times Exxon Mobil's 2011 profits. On the other hand, a staggering $107 billion—about four times BP's 2011 profits[3]—left the states with the highest income taxes.

Let's look at another correlation, measured by per capita state-local tax burdens. Per capita state-local tax burdens include all of the state and local taxes—including income taxes, property taxes, sales taxes, etc.—paid by residents. We use the most recent findings from the Washington, DC-based Tax Foundation's "Annual State-Local Tax Burden Ranking," a comprehensive state-by-state study of the taxes paid by residents of all 50 states and the District of Columbia.[4] Here are the income numbers for the states with the *lowest* per capita state taxes and the *highest.*

The 10 states with the *lowest* state-local tax burdens per capita (the national average is 9.9 percent):

RANK	STATE	PER CAPITA TAX BURDEN	NET GAIN (OR LOSS)
1	Alaska	7%	($1.4 billion)
2	South Dakota	7.6%	$528 million
3	Tennessee	7.7%	$8.3 billion
4	Louisiana	7.8%	($6.1 billion)
5	Wyoming	7.9%	$1.3 billion
6	Texas	7.9%	$22.1 billion
7	New Hampshire	8.1%	$3.2 billion
8	Alabama	8.2%	$13 billion
9	Nevada	8.2%	$16 billion
10	South Carolina	8.4%	$13 billion
			Total gain all 10: $69.9 billion

The 10 states with the *highest* state-local tax burdens per capita (the national average is 9.9 percent):

RANK	STATE	PER CAPITA TAX BURDEN	NET GAIN (OR LOSS)
1	New York	12.8%	($58.6 billion)
2	New Jersey	12.4%	($18.5 billion)
3	Connecticut	12.3%	($6.1 billion)
4	California	11.2%	($31.8 billion)
5	Wisconsin	11.1%	($2.5 billion)
6	Rhode Island	10.9%	($1.2 billion)
7	Minnesota	10.8%	($4.1 billion)
8	Massachusetts	10.4%	($10.8 billion)
9	Maine	10.3%	$1.6 billion
10	Pennsylvania	10.2%	($7 billion)
			Total loss all 10: $139 billion

Pretty amazing. Again we see that the states with the lowest tax regimes gained the most in net AGI while the states with the highest per capita tax burdens lost massive amounts.

~

In the digital age, geography matters less and less. We can work from anywhere, we can shop from anywhere, and we can access the same information from anywhere. We are personally and professionally mobile. The digital age demands—and encourages—mobility, but that mobility is in conflict with rigid tax codes not designed for our mobile lifestyles. If you can work from anywhere, why would you work in a state with high personal income tax rates? The mobility of the digital age means our choices are far less limited.

On the other hand, geography matters a great deal when it comes to weather, certain jobs, and cultural and lifestyle factors, all of which weigh heavily in a person's choice of where to live. Lifestyle will often dictate—more than any other factor—where a person chooses to live. If you want to break into country music, you're probably better off living in Nashville than Cleveland. If you want to surf every day, you might not want to pick Chicago. If you are strongly committed to your lifestyle your choices are limited.

There is another issue that is still very much geographic: taxes. Aside from federal income taxes—which you pay no matter where you live—the local and state income and other taxes you pay are very much predicated on where you live. We may be mobile, but we still pay taxes based on where we live. And that matters a great deal. If you live in Nevada, for example, you do not pay state personal income taxes. If you live in California you could pay the highest in the country, up to 13.3 percent.

FEDERAL TAXES	STATE/LOCAL TAXES
Location: Fixed	Location: Variable *Consumer choices!*

In terms of state personal income taxes, it matters where you live. So, for the sake of argument, if you have mobility, if you can work from anywhere, wouldn't you choose to live where you can keep more of what you earn? That is, wouldn't you choose to live where taxes are low? And if those places also happen to be where the opportunity is, where there is a growing local economy...bam! You have the perfect economic-opportunity cocktail.

Taxes are very important. Corporations make major decisions based on tax regimes. Very often, they locate their headquarters and various operations where the taxes are low. For example, Texas is home to some of the biggest corporations in the world. Why? Perhaps because the state has no personal income taxes and the fifth lowest state-local per capita tax burden in the country, at 7.9 percent, according to the Tax Foundation. Smart money moves to Texas.

Other taxes play a big role in corporate decisions, too. For example, Facebook, Google, Apple, and Amazon have all constructed enormous data centers in Oregon. Why? Though Oregon has a top state income tax rate of 9.9 percent and a per capita state-local tax burden of 10 percent, it has no sales tax (it's one of only five states in the U.S. with no sales tax). As Jay Park, who heads design, construction, and operations for Facebook's data centers put it to *The Economist*: "You replace a server every three years and a server costs a lot, so sales tax is a big deal."[5]

Incentives matter. Corporations take tax issues into consideration all the time. Why wouldn't people do the same? Why wouldn't tax issues—particularly personal income taxes—be a major factor in deciding where to live? Why wouldn't money walk to where it is most welcome? Actually, I think it already does.

~

Let's do a little math to find out how much more of your income you could keep by living in a state with no income tax. We'll take a look at two hypothetical households, the Smiths in San Francisco and the Millers in Miami. For the sake of argument, we will assume they are identical in every way except for where they live. Both families make $250,000. For the sake of simplicity, we are going to leave off all deductions and exemptions—like real estate taxes, mortgage interest, children, etc.—and just take the standard exemption and deduction.

The Smiths of California

Wages: $250,000

Less California standard exemption: $208
Less California standard deduction: $7,682

California Taxable Income = $242,110

Their California marginal tax rate would be 9.3 percent. (The top personal income tax rate of 13.3 percent starts at $1 million in annual income and above.)

Their income taxes to California: $17,772.68[6]

The Millers of Miami

Wages: $250,000

There are no deductions at the state level because Florida has no state personal income tax.

Their income taxes to the state of Florida: zero

The Millers get to keep $17,772.68 more of their money.

But the Millers of Miami would also likely get to keep even more of their income because they would also pay lower sales taxes–California's state sales tax rate is 7.25 percent whereas Florida's is 6 percent—and, according to the Tax Foundation, California has the fourth highest state-local tax burden in the country, at 11.2 percent. Florida ranks 27th in the country with a state-local tax burden of just 9.3 percent, below the national average of 9.9 percent.

Now, this is obviously a very simple equation done strictly for the purposes of showing how much more of your income you could keep if you lived in a state with no personal income taxes. It's simplified a great deal, but it is still accurate. If you were the Millers you would not have to pay any state personal income tax in Florida, so, in this example, you would get to keep about $17,772 more of your income.

MILLERS' LIFE	SMITHS' LIFE
+$17,772 every year Options!	[Flat]

Regardless of your income bracket, $17,772 is a lot of money. That's enough to buy a decent car, put a down payment on a house, or pay for a year's tuition with room, board, and books at the University of Florida.[7]

UNIVERSITY OF FLORIDA	UNIVERSITY OF CALIFORNIA
Tuition, room, board, and books: $16,620	Tuition, room, board, and books: $28,200

In just 10 years, the Millers would get to keep $177,720 more of their own income just by virtue of where they live. Whether they spend it, save it, invest it, start a business, build a swimming pool, travel the world, it is money—their own income—that they get to keep (or have the option to keep) solely by living in Florida, a state with no personal income taxes. If you had an extra $17,772 a year, what would you do with it?

Now, did our hypothetical Millers choose to live in Florida for that reason? Or did they move there so they wouldn't have to pay income taxes? Who knows; they are a hypothetical family, after all. Nevertheless, the money people get to keep when they live in states with no personal income tax is real. What they do with it is up to them, and it's an opportunity based solely on where they live. This raises a host of questions: Who takes (and took) advantage of these opportunities? If the savings are so stark, and the incentive so great, why didn't we see even more movement? Why don't more people move?

~

The answers may go back to the premise we discussed in the last chapter—rational ignorance. Remember, rational ignorance means avoiding something that you feel is inherently negative, or avoiding an action that you feel you cannot likely or easily change.

Our reaction to income taxes is (for most of us) a perfect example of rational ignorance at work. We know we pay federal income taxes (that's the rational part), but we are often willfully ignorant of how much we pay. We may not even know the total amount we pay in a given year. We have to pay incomes taxes; we have no choice. For most people, the money is taken before we even see it (this is by design, by the way). We may spend a few seconds fuming when we get our pay stubs, but we never held that money in our hands, so our brain tells us to move on and worry about being attacked by a shark instead.

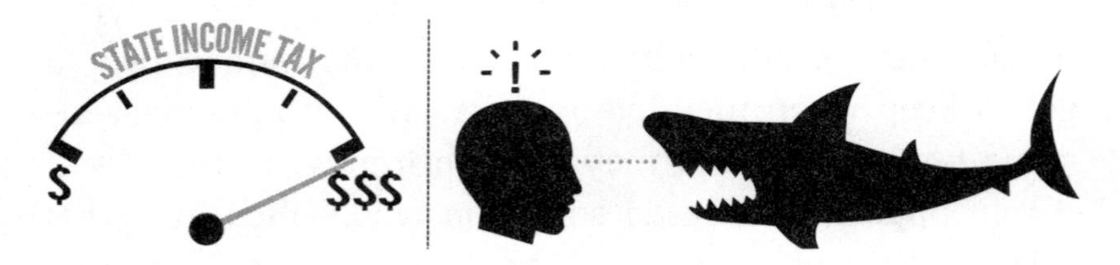

Now, you have a one in 11.5 million chance of being attacked by a shark, but, if you're reading this book, you probably have a 100 percent chance of paying federal income taxes. However, because we have no choice in the matter and we can't change it, we ignore it and move on. That's rational ignorance, and that's why, as a general rule, we do not take the time to crunch the numbers and find out how much we are paying in income taxes every year. And we certainly don't take the time to find out how much more or less we would pay if we moved to another state.

It may be rational ignorance, but it is also just too hard to calculate your taxes given the complexity of the federal tax code, plus any state or local taxes. The simple federal tax code of 100 years ago has ballooned to a monster that only professionals can figure out. "What began 99 years ago as a three-page income tax form with one page of instructions has evolved into a monstrosity with more than 500 separate tax forms," wrote Burton Abrams, professor of economics at the University of Delaware. "Tax-preparation instructions now exceed a staggering 7,000 pages. In 2009 alone, according to Internal Revenue Service estimates, taxpayers hired as many as 1.2 million paid tax-preparers to help break through the morass of tax rules."[8] No wonder we ignore income taxes.

Furthermore, the intuitive brain is concerned primarily with frequency—the price of gas because we drive every day, the price of milk because we have six kids—or high-impact dramas—such as a plane crash, a shark attack, etc. Our thoughts tend to focus on items like these, things that are of high impact but low probability, or, conversely, things we can directly control or change.

Because your income tax is removed before you even see it (again, by design) you feel you have no choice in the matter, which, in the case of federal taxes, is largely true. However, there is a great deal of choice when it comes to state personal income taxes. Federal income taxes are fixed. They fluctuate based on the size of income, deductions, exemptions, etc., but you pay them no matter where you live. State income taxes, however, vary widely, and I believe that the people who have a high perception of their freedom to choose are the ones who take advantage and move.

Choice and impact are intuitive decisions, and an action happens at the intersection of impact and choice. If you feel you have a choice and the impact is positive, you take action. If you feel you have no choice and the impact is marginal, you do nothing. Moving is hard. There are a lot of obstacles to exercising that choice, so it's easy to see why people don't do it. The infrequency of paying income taxes, combined with the burden of displacement and the emotional anxiety and hassle of moving add up to inertia. Who wants the hassle?

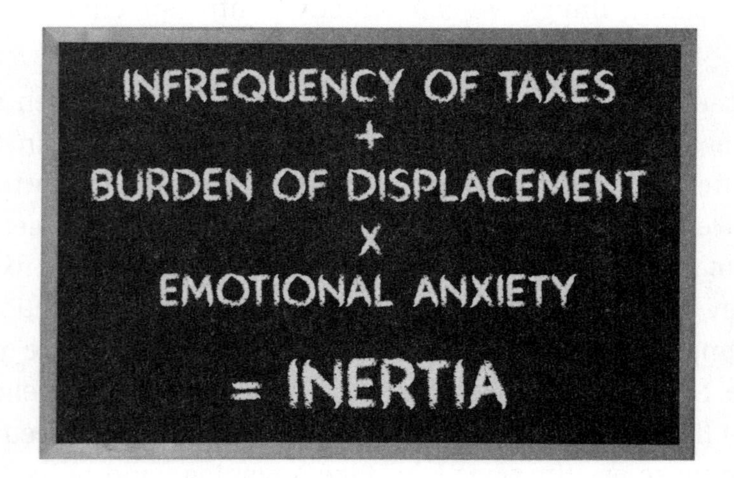

But this perception changes depending on one's income level. Often, people with high incomes perceive a high degree of choice and mobility and perceive (rightly) that a move will have a high financial impact. People with low incomes perceive a low degree of choice and mobility and perceive (wrongly) that a move will have a low financial impact. So the people who move are the ones who see a high degree of choice and a high impact.

For many of us, the choices seem nonexistent ("I have to pay income taxes"), the impact seems low ("How much can I really save?"), and the benefits uncertain ("Will they impose an income tax after I move? And what if I can't find a job?"). So our gut tells us not to do anything. We are hardwired for stasis, for maintaining the status quo. We choose an immediate benefit (staying put), over a long-term gain (moving).

But high-income earners figured this out years ago. They have always been adept at preventing a far greater amount of their income from being taxed, either through deferrals or living in states with no income taxes. But now, with the IRS data we mapped, we see that more people, not just millionaires, are moving. In fact, when you average the AGI that moved, the incomes are fairly modest. Here are the average incomes that moved into the 10 states that saw the greatest gains:

1. FLORIDA	
	Net gain: $86.4 billion
	Average AGI: $52,123

2. ARIZONA	
	Net gain: $24.5 billion
	Average AGI: $44,479

3. TEXAS	
	Net gain: $22.1 billion
	Average AGI: $43,745

4. NORTH CAROLINA	
	Net gain: $21.6 billion
	Average AGI: $42,546

5. NEVADA	
	Net gain: $16 billion
	Average AGI: $44,639

6. SOUTH CAROLINA	
	Net gain: $13 billion
	Average AGI: $44,205

7. GEORGIA	
	Net gain: $12.4 billion
	Average AGI: $38,705

8. COLORADO	
	Net gain: $11 billion
	Average AGI: $45,234

9. WASHINGTON	
	Net gain: $9.9 billion
	Average AGI: $44,254

10. TENNESSEE	
	Net gain: $8.3 billion
	Average AGI: $39,960

Are they millionaires? No. Did they move because they knew they could save more of their income? Who knows? The data only shows AGI, which we can average based on population migration figures. The rest is speculative. But when it comes to accumulating wealth, there are a few tried and true factors.

~

In *The Millionaire Next Door: The Surprising Secrets of America's Wealthy*, authors Thomas Stanley and William Danko share the common practices of people who have a lot of wealth. First, the authors define wealth: it is what you accumulate, not what you spend. In their decades of studying wealthy people, they found that "Wealth is more often the result of a lifestyle of hard work, perseverance, planning, and, most of all, self-discipline."[9]

It takes a lot to become a millionaire. Wealthy people make the smart and sometimes harder choices. They work hard, they're frugal, they have the right job in the right market, they're smart with the way they handle and invest their money, and so on. They accumulate wealth as a result of their choices. But it all comes down to this: they accumulate wealth by keeping more of what they earn. And what is one of the best ways to keep more of what you earn? Pay less in income taxes.

STATES WITH NO INCOME TAX	STATES WITH HIGH INCOME TAX
More savings = Greater net worth	Higher taxes = Lower net worth
Greater net worth = Greater options to save, spend, or invest	Lower net worth = Fewer options to save, spend, or invest
Greater options = Greater wealth	Fewer options = Less wealth

Yes, frugality tops the authors' list of the seven common denominators of the truly wealthy as a way to keep more of what you earn (hint: don't spend it), but an obvious way to keep more of your own income is to not pay it in income taxes. Now, there are all sorts of deductions and exemptions and tax-deferred instruments to lower your income taxes at the federal level, but at the state level, one of the easiest things to do to keep more of your income is to live in a state with no income taxes. Remember the Smiths and the Millers? All things being equal, which family stands to gain greater wealth over the long run? The one that has the most income to start with, which means the family that pays no state income taxes.

It's a lot easier to be wealthier (maybe even a millionaire) if you live in a state with no income taxes. Among the many, many factors that lead to real wealth, minimizing the income tax you pay is one of the most significant and obvious. Then, what you do with money is, of course, up to you. But wealthy people are smart about their money. They make choices that allow them to keep more of what they earn.

So, does this mean that the people who moved understood the concept of accumulating wealth? Not necessarily. Does this mean that all the people who migrated are millionaires who are just trying to keep more of their money? No. As we saw, the AGIs per person are fairly modest. Does it mean that once people secure something of value–in this case personal income–they move to places where they can keep more of it? Maybe. That would be an obvious deduction, but one that cannot be proven from our data. Does it mean the people who have migrated are on the road to getting rich? No. Again, we cannot prove that from the data.

Does it mean that the cause of the migration is the high tax regimes in some states and the low ones in others? Maybe. There is a certain romance in singling out a variable and any one of the above is tempting. People look for the easiest and most obvious factor, but my intent is merely to map the data and offer a few possibilities.

However, we do know a few things. First, if you live in a state with no personal income taxes you get to keep more of your personal income. Second, when you tax something you get less of it. Third, $2 trillion in adjusted gross income moved between the states between 1995 and 2010. And fourth, that income migrated from high-tax states to low-tax ones. The states with the highest personal income and per capita taxes saw the most precipitous drops in AGI (the money that is eligible to be taxed), while the states with no or low income taxes enjoyed massive influxes of working wealth.

This chapter (or the book, for that matter) is not intended to be a primer on getting rich. Nor am I saying that all the smart, wealthy people move to states with no income taxes. You will not get rich just because you live in a state with no income taxes. But if you are savvy and are seeking opportunity, you could do worse than move to a state with no income tax. Those are the states with economies that are growing. Those are the states that allow you to keep more of what you earn in your own pocket. Do with it what you will, but letting you keep more of your own money and giving you the choice of how to spend it is a key factor in growth, as well as personal opportunity.

It's all about choice. And it's all about moving beyond rational ignorance into a true understanding of how wealth works, how personal income taxes affect your accumulation of wealth (and the economy as a whole), and how you can exercise choice.

So, millions of people made the choice to move. Did they move for tax reasons? Did they move for a perceived benefit? An opportunity or incentive? Almost certainly. They left some states and flocked to others, taking $2 trillion in adjusted gross income with them. So, where did they go? Let's take a look.

Scan here for supplemental and additional material, illustrations, video, and other information.

Chapter Two Endnotes:

[1] Samuel Stouffer, *American Sociological Review* (December 1940), p. 846.

[2] Michael J. Graetz, *100 Million Unnecessary Returns* (New Haven: Yale University Press, 2008), p. 212.

[3] Both revenue figures from "The World's Biggest Public Companies," Forbes.com (April 18, 2012), http://www.forbes.com/global2000/list/.

[4] Here and throughout the book, Elizabeth Malm and Gerald Prante, "Annual State-Local Tax Burden Ranking," Background Paper No. 65 (October 2012), the Tax Foundation, http://www.taxfoundation.org/sites/taxfoundation.org/files/docs/BP65_2010_Burdens_Report.pdf.

[5] "Not a cloud in sight," Special Report on Technology and Geography, *The Economist* (Oct. 27, 2012), p. 20.

[6] A small part of the Smiths's state income tax could potentially be offset by a reduction of their federal tax liability due to the deductibility of state income taxes when calculating federal taxable income. However, the ability to take advantage of this deduction depends on other deductions the Smiths may have, as well as the limitations of the Alternative Minimum Tax. California tax rates and exemptions, https://www.ftb.ca.gov/forms/2012_California_Tax_Rates_and_Exemptions.shtml.

[7] University of Florida cost of attendance 2012-2013 school year, http://www.sfa.ufl.edu/basics/cost-of-attendance/; University of California cost of attendance 2012-2013 school year, http://admission.universityofcalifornia.edu/paying-for-uc/cost/index.html.

[8] Burton A. Abrams, "Celebrate the Income Tax's 100th Birthday by Fixing It" (September 17, 2012), http://www.independent.org/newsroom/article.asp?id=3431.

[9] Thomas J. Stanley and William D. Danko, *The Millionaire Next Door: The Surprising Secrets of America's Wealthy* (Atlanta: Longstreet Press, 1996), p. 2.

Chapter Three

A LOOK AT THE STATES AND METROPOLITAN AREAS

Winners, losers, and how their taxes stack up

We know that a massive movement of working wealth took place between 1995 and 2010, and when we map the data we get a startling picture of bright reds (where the aggregate income came from), deep greens (where the aggregate income landed), and various shades in between (go to www.howmoneywalks.com to see the map).

Let's begin with a macro view of the states to get a big idea of who is "winning" and who is "losing" when it comes to income migration. From there, we will drill down to the local level, to the metropolitan statistical areas (MSAs) and the counties.

Aggregate income migration information and full reports on all 50 states, the District of Columbia, every county in America, and the top and bottom 20 MSAs is available on my Web site, www.howmoneywalks.com. The information on the Web site is incredibly detailed and is mapped by state, county, and MSA for ease of use. With a simple click, you can see how each state, county, and major MSA fared from 1995 to 2010, how much adjusted gross income (AGI)—as reported on federal 1040 forms to the IRS—moved into or out of the entity, and where the income came from or where it went.

In this chapter, I want to provide an overview of the national trend we are seeing from this data mapping, so I am going to provide information on the top 10 state gainers and losers, and then do the same for the top and bottom 10 MSAs. Then, in later chapters, we will look closely at each MSA.

Now, I hate to use the term "loser," and I mean no disrespect. By loser I simply mean that the state or MSA lost aggregate income, nothing more. There is no judgment in that term; it simply means a net loss of AGI due to migration.

For each of the state gainers and losers I list the cumulative net change in AGI (a gain or a loss) as reported by actual taxpayers to the IRS on federal 1040 forms. This is reported aggregate income, and this is the money that is moving from place to place that we mapped over a 15-year period, 1995-2010.

To provide as complete a picture as possible for the states, I am also providing:

- The top five states from which each state gained or lost AGI
- The cumulative population gain or loss in that state

- The state's top marginal income tax rate
- The state-local tax burden (the U.S. average is 9.9 percent)
- The taxes paid per capita (the U.S. average is $4,112)
- The state's national tax burden ranking

The rankings are based on the state and local tax burdens and are ranked from the highest overall tax burden in the nation (1), to the lowest (50). Again, the population figures are from the Census Bureau and the last three items are taken from the Washington, DC-based Tax Foundation's annual report and rankings.[1]

Here are the 10 states that saw the greatest net gain of AGI, 1995-2010:

1. FLORIDA	
Net gain of AGI	$86.4 billion
Top five states from which Florida gained AGI	New York - $16.8 billion New Jersey - $10.2 billion Illinois - $6.2 billion Ohio - $5.9 billion Pennsylvania - $5.7 billion
Cumulative population gain	905,856
Top state income tax rate	0%
State-local tax burden	9.3%
Taxes per capita	$3,728
Rank	27

2. ARIZONA

Net gain of AGI	$24.5 billion
Top five states from which Arizona gained AGI	California - $6.3 billion Illinois - $2.5 billion New York - $1.4 billion Michigan - $1.2 billion Minnesota - $1 billion
Cumulative population gain	441,749
Top state income tax rate	4.54%
State-local tax burden	8.4%
Taxes per capita	$3,006
Rank	40

3. TEXAS

Net gain of AGI	$22.1 billion
Top five states from which Texas gained AGI	California - $4.8 billion Louisiana - $3 billion Illinois - $2 billion New York - $1.6 billion Michigan - $1.2 billion
Cumulative population gain	543,557
Top state income tax rate	0%
State-local tax burden	7.9%
Taxes per capita	$3,104
Rank	45

4. NORTH CAROLINA	
Net gain of AGI	$21.6 billion
Top five states from which North Carolina gained AGI	New York - $4 billion New Jersey - $2.3 billion Virginia - $2 billion Pennsylvania - $1.6 billion California - $1.4 billion
Cumulative population gain	419,636
Top state income tax rate	7.75%
State-local tax burden	9.9%
Taxes per capita	$3,535
Rank	17

5. NEVADA	
Net gain of AGI	$16 billion
Top five states from which Nevada gained AGI	California - $8.2 billion Illinois - $924 million New York - $896 million Michigan - $531 million Ohio - $463 million
Cumulative population gain	274,991
Top state income tax rate	0%
State-local tax burden	8.2%
Taxes per capita	$3,297
Rank	42

6. SOUTH CAROLINA

Net gain of AGI	$13 billion
Top five states from which South Carolina gained AGI	New York - $1.8 billion New Jersey - $1.3 billion North Carolina - $1.2 billion Ohio - $1.1 billion Pennsylvania - $970 million
Cumulative population gain	176,053
Top state income tax rate	7%
State-local tax burden	8.4%
Taxes per capita	$2,760
Rank	41

7. GEORGIA

Net gain of AGI	$12.4 billion
Top five states from which Georgia gained AGI	New York - $2 billion New Jersey - $1.2 billion Illinois - $829 million Ohio - $810 million Michigan - $779 million
Cumulative population gain	519,998
Top state income tax rate	6%
State-local tax burden	9%
Taxes per capita	$3,222
Rank	33

8. COLORADO	
Net gain of AGI	$11 billion
Top five states from which Colorado gained AGI	California - $3 billion Illinois - $1.3 billion Texas - $934 million New York - $637 million Ohio - $532 million
Cumulative population gain	202,515
Top state income tax rate	4.63%
State-local tax burden	9.1%
Taxes per capita	$4,104
Rank	32

9. WASHINGTON	
Net gain of AGI	$9.9 billion
Top five states from which Washington gained AGI	California - $4 billion Oregon - $2 billion Illinois - $493 million New York - $441 million Alaska - $430 million
Cumulative population gain	169,313
Top state income tax rate	0%
State-local tax burden	9.3%
Taxes per capita	$4,261
Rank	28

10. TENNESSEE	
Net gain of AGI	$8.3 billion
Top five states from which Tennessee gained AGI	California - $926 million Michigan - $846 million Illinois - $797 million Florida - $711 million Ohio - $643 million
Cumulative population gain	185,026
Top state income tax rate	0%
State-local tax burden	7.7%
Taxes per capita	$2,707
Rank	48

Total gain top 10: $2.25 trillion

And here are the 10 states that saw the greatest net loss of AGI, 1995-2010:

1. NEW YORK	
Net loss of AGI	$58.6 billion
Top five states to which New York lost AGI	Florida - $16.8 billion New Jersey - $11.6 billion Connecticut - $5.4 billion North Carolina - $4 billion California - $3.3 billion
Cumulative population loss	771,736
Top state income tax rate	8.82%
State-local tax burden	12.8%
Taxes per capita	$6,375
Rank	1 (highest in the nation)

2. CALIFORNIA	
Net loss of AGI	$31.8 billion
Top five states to which California lost AGI	Nevada - $8.2 billion Arizona - $6.3 billion Oregon - $4.9 billion Texas - $4.9 billion Washington - $3.9 billion
Cumulative population loss	340,662
Top state income tax rate	13.3%
State-local tax burden	11.2%
Taxes per capita	$4,934
Rank	4

3. ILLINOIS

3. ILLINOIS	
Net loss of AGI	$26.1 billion
Top five states to which Illinois lost AGI	Florida - $6.2 billion California - $2.5 billion Arizona - $2.5 billion Texas - $2 billion Wisconsin - $1.9 billion
Cumulative population loss	299,889
Top state income tax rate	5%
State-local tax burden	10.2%
Taxes per capita	$4,512
Rank	11

4. NEW JERSEY

4. NEW JERSEY	
Net loss of AGI	$18.5 billion
Top five states to which New Jersey lost AGI	Florida - $10.2 billion Pennsylvania - $2.7 billion North Carolina - $2.3 billion California - $1.8 billion Virginia - $1.5 billion
Cumulative population loss	238,174
Top state income tax rate	8.97%
State-local tax burden	12.4%
Taxes per capita	$6,689
Rank	2

5. OHIO

Net loss of AGI	$17.1 billion
Top five states to which Ohio lost AGI	Florida - $5.9 billion North Carolina - $1.6 billion Texas - $1.1 billion South Carolina - $1.1 billion Arizona - $1 billion
Cumulative population loss	242,039
Top state income tax rate	5.93%
State-local tax burden	9.7%
Taxes per capita	$3,563
Rank	20

6. MICHIGAN

Net loss of AGI	$15.6 billion
Top five states to which Michigan lost AGI	Florida - $4.8 billion California - $1.3 billion Texas - $1.2 billion Arizona - $1.2 billion North Carolina - $1 billion
Cumulative population loss	247,878
Top state income tax rate	4.35%
State-local tax burden	9.8%
Taxes per capita	$3,503
Rank	18

7. MASSACHUSETTS

Net loss of AGI	$10.8 billion
Top five states to which Massachusetts lost AGI	Florida - $4.7 billion New Hampshire - $2.9 billion California - $1.4 billion Maine - $806 million North Carolina - $756 million
Cumulative population loss	98,869
Top state income tax rate	5.3%
State-local tax burden	10.4%
Taxes per capita	$5,422
Rank	8

8. PENNSYLVANIA

Net loss of AGI	$6.9 billion
Top five states to which Pennsylvania lost AGI	Florida - $6.9 billion North Carolina - $1.6 billion South Carolina - $970 million California - $772 million Virginia - $739 million
Cumulative population loss	123,072
Top state income tax rate	3.07%
State-local tax burden	10.2%
Taxes per capita	$4,183
Rank	10

9. MARYLAND	
Net loss of AGI	$6.5 billion
Top five states to which Maryland lost AGI	Florida - $3.7 billion North Carolina - $1.2 billion Virginia - $1.1 billion Pennsylvania - $999 million West Virginia - $626 million
Cumulative population loss	10,294
Top state income tax rate	5.5%
State-local tax burden	10.2%
Taxes per capita	$5,234
Rank	12

10. CONNECTICUT	
Net loss of AGI	$6.1 billion
Top five states to which Connecticut lost AGI	Florida - $4.3 billion North Carolina - $946 million Massachusetts - $892 million Virginia - $676 million California - $574 million
Cumulative population loss	89,064
Top state income tax rate	6.7%
State-local tax burden	12.3%
Taxes per capita	$6,984
Rank	3

Total loss for those 10 states: $198 billion.

Pretty staggering. Overall, more than $2 trillion of adjusted gross income moved between the states between 1995 and 2010, yet this is a little-discussed event. Perhaps it's because it happened gradually, over many years, and it is only when the data is organized, mapped, and presented that the trend lines emerge and the full view of the movement is seen. Perhaps, as we discussed in the preceding chapter, it's because we have other things on our minds. Maybe we don't want to know about this. Whatever the case, we know now.

~

But the movement begs the big question, why? Why did aggregate income move in such huge numbers to some states and flee others? Why did Florida, Arizona, Texas, North Carolina, and Nevada gain such huge numbers while New York, California, Illinois, New Jersey, and Ohio lose staggering sums?

Did people move because of the weather? A job? Family? School? Retirement? Undoubtedly, many factors come into play, but people don't just move on a whim. Moving is a big deal. It's a hassle. It takes time and money and lots of effort. So, as we discussed in the last chapter, we can surmise that people move for a real reason or set of reasons. What those reasons are may not be altogether clear, but when we look at the data behind the movement we see a pattern. The states that saw the greatest net gains in AGI and people have something in common: they have no or low state personal income taxes or relatively low state tax burdens.

Conversely, the states that lost the most AGI have high-to-very-high state personal income tax rates and moderate-to-high state tax burdens per capita. More and more, it looks like taxes matter. We know, empirically, that millions of people and billions of dollars in adjusted gross incomes are moving every year. And we may be seeing one of the reasons why.

Let's break it down even more and take a look at income movement based on two different but related categories: first, state personal income tax rates and, second, state per capita tax burdens.

There are nine states with no state personal income taxes. Based, again, on information from the IRS Division of Statistics, here are the stats for 1995-2010 for those nine states, along with the stats from the nine states with the highest state personal income tax rates:

The nine states with *zero* state personal income taxes:

1. Alaska	LOST $1.4 billion
2. Florida	GAINED $86.4 billion
3. New Hampshire	GAINED $3.2 billion
4. Nevada	GAINED $16 billion
5. South Dakota	GAINED $528 million
6. Tennessee	GAINED $8.3 billion
7. Texas	GAINED $22 billion
8. Washington	GAINED $9.9 billion
9. Wyoming	GAINED $1.3 billion
TOTAL	***GAINED $146.2 billion***

The nine states with the *highest* personal income tax rates:

1. California (13.3%)	LOST $31.8 billion
2. Hawaii (11%)	GAINED $198 million
3. Oregon (9.9%)	GAINED $5.6 billion
4. Iowa (8.98%)	LOST $3.2 billion
5. New Jersey (8.97%)	LOST $18.5 billion
6. Vermont (8.95%)	GAINED $693 million
7. Washington, DC (8.9%)	LOST $3.4 billion
8. New York (8.82%)	LOST $58.6 billion
9. Maine (8.5%)	GAINED $1.6 billion
TOTAL	***LOST $107.4 billion***

Of the states with no personal income taxes, only Alaska saw a loss of aggregate income. The other eight states gained, together, over $140 billion. That's the market value of the massive pharmaceutical company Merck, which makes Claritin, Coppertone, Pepcid AC, and Propecia.[2]

Of those states with the highest personal income tax rates, only three enjoyed a gain, while six saw the loss of $115 billion in aggregate income, roughly the market value of Amazon.[3]

Now let's look at state and local tax burden per capita, another potential marker for migration. State and local tax burdens per capita include all the state and local taxes a person pays, including personal income tax, sales tax, etc. Again, the rankings are taken from the Tax Foundation's most recent report, and the states are ranked from the highest state-local tax burden per capita in the country (1) to the lowest (50). I have included AGI figures as well.

The 10 states with the *highest* state-local tax burdens:

1. New York	LOST $58.6 billion
2. New Jersey	LOST $18.5 billion
3. Connecticut	LOST $6.1 billion
4. California	LOST $31.8 billion
5. Wisconsin	LOST $2.5 billion
6. Rhode Island	LOST $1.2 billion
7. Minnesota	LOST $4.1 billion
8. Massachusetts	LOST $10.8 billion
9. Maine	GAINED $1.6 billion
10. Pennsylvania	LOST $7 billion
TOTAL LOSS ALL 10	***$139 billion***

The 10 states with the *lowest* state-local tax burdens:

1. Alaska	LOST $1.4 billion
2. South Dakota	GAINED $528 million
3. Tennessee	GAINED $8.3 billion
4. Louisiana	LOST $6.1 billion
5. Wyoming	GAINED $1.3 billion
6. Texas	GAINED $22.1 billion
7. New Hampshire	GAINED $3.2 billion
8. Alabama	GAINED $13 billion
9. Nevada	GAINED $16 billion
10. South Carolina	GAINED $13 billion
TOTAL GAIN ALL 10	***$69.9 billion***

Nine of the 10 states with the highest per capita tax burdens saw a precipitous outward migration of income totaling a massive $139 billion. That's about 10 times what Google earned in 2011.[4] But the states with the *lowest* state tax burdens saw a gain in aggregate income of almost $70 billion, twice the market value of Nike.[5]

Can we conclude that low to no state income taxes or low per capita state tax burdens are the reason for income migration? Not necessarily. Again, there is likely no single factor at play here. However, there is a clear and unmistakable migration pattern of aggregate income *from* high-tax states *to* low-tax states, especially when you consider personal income tax rates.

And this goes for MSAs, as well. Now, MSAs are trickier because some MSAs—like New York and Washington, DC—encompass areas in more than one state.[6] However, if you look at the 10 MSAs that gained the most AGI, they are all in single states, and six of those 10 are in states with no income taxes. Conversely, the 10 MSAs that *lost* the most AGI are in states with high personal income taxes or high state-local tax burdens.

The 10 MSAs that *gained* the most AGI, 1995-2010:

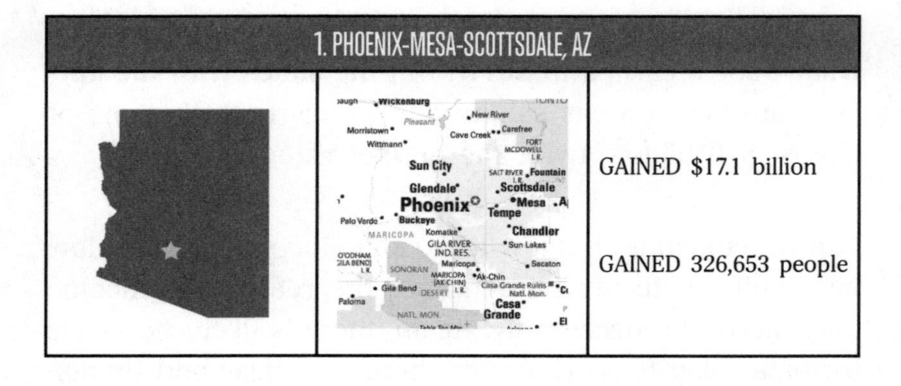

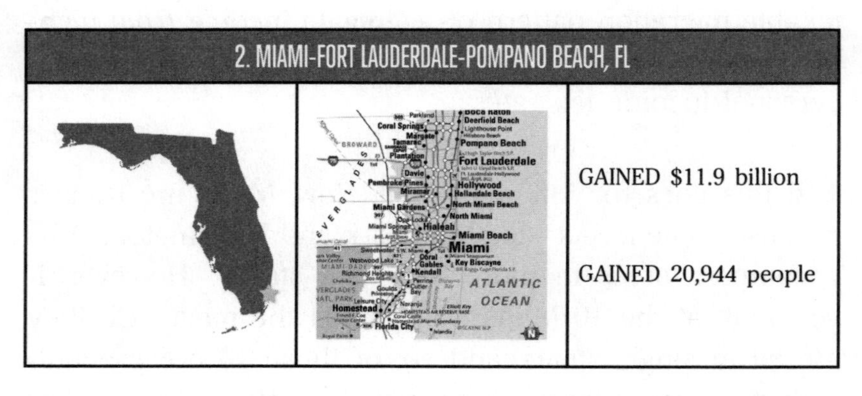

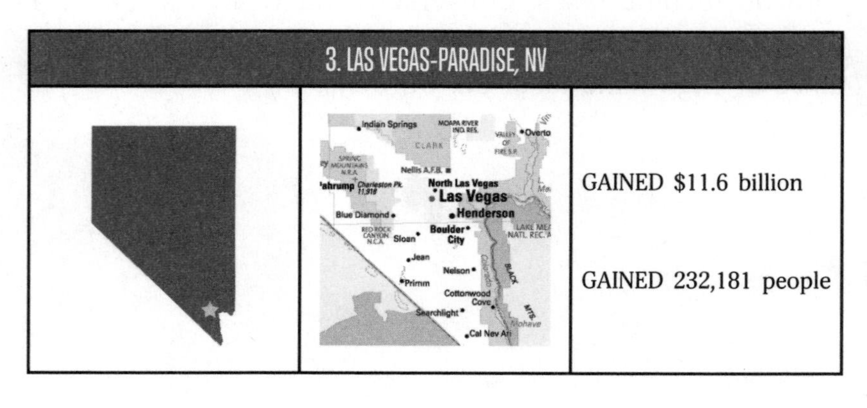

4. RIVERSIDE-SAN BERNARDINO-ONTARIO, CA

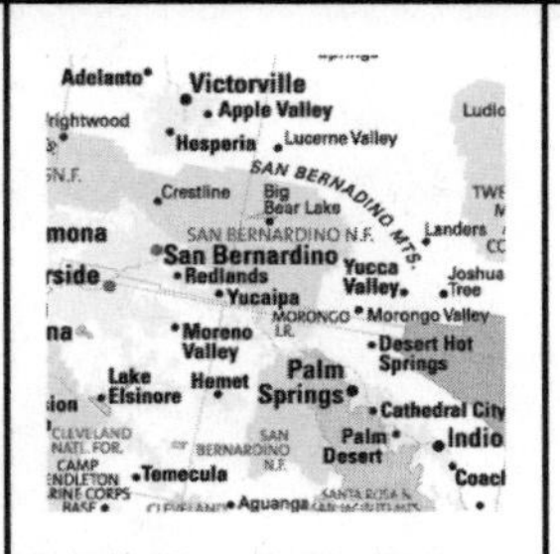

GAINED $11.1 billion

GAINED 202,606 people

5. NAPLES-MARCO ISLAND, FL

GAINED $10.1 billion

GAINED 31,745 people

6. TAMPA-ST. PETERSBURG-CLEARWATER, FL

GAINED $9.8 billion

GAINED 185,711 people

7. CAPE CORAL-FORT MYERS, FL

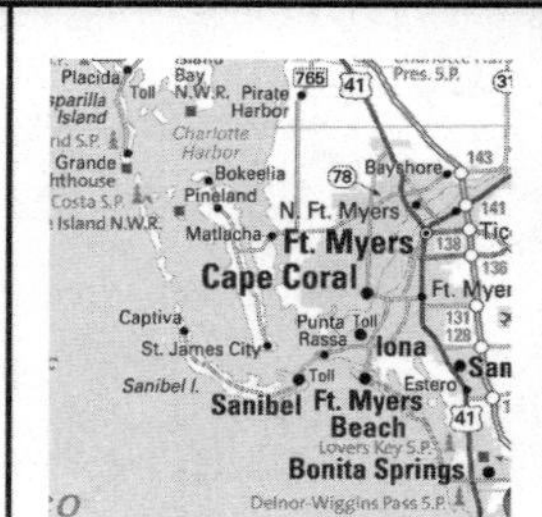

GAINED $9 billion

GAINED 80,036 people

GAINED $9 billion

GAINED 426,069 people

9. NORTH PORT-BRADENTON-SARASOTA, FL

GAINED $8.8 billion

GAINED 70,324 people

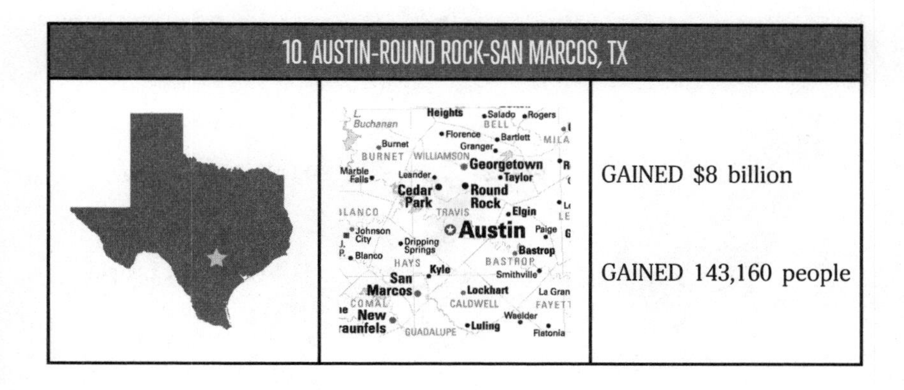

Total gain top 10: $106.4 billion

The 10 MSAs that *lost* the most AGI, 1995-2010:

2. LOS ANGELES-LONG BEACH-SANTA ANA, CA

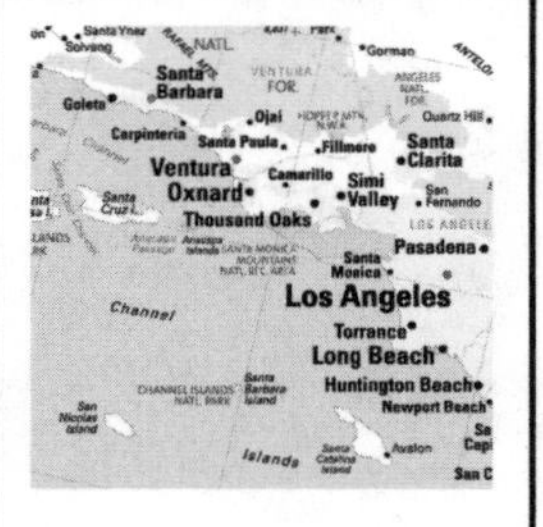

LOST $31.5 billion

LOST 494,800 people

3. CHICAGO-NAPERVILLE-JOLIET, IL, IN, WI

LOST $21.1 billion

LOST 211,623 people

4. DETROIT-WARREN-LIVONIA, MI

LOST $12.5 billion

LOST 178,118 people

5. SAN JOSE-SUNNYVALE-SANTA CLARA, CA

LOST $12.3 billion

LOST 80,452 people

6. WASHINGTON-ARLINGTON-ALEXANDRIA, DC, VA, MD, WV

LOST $11.3 billion

GAINED 55,424 people

7. BOSTON-CAMBRIDGE-QUINCY, MA, NH

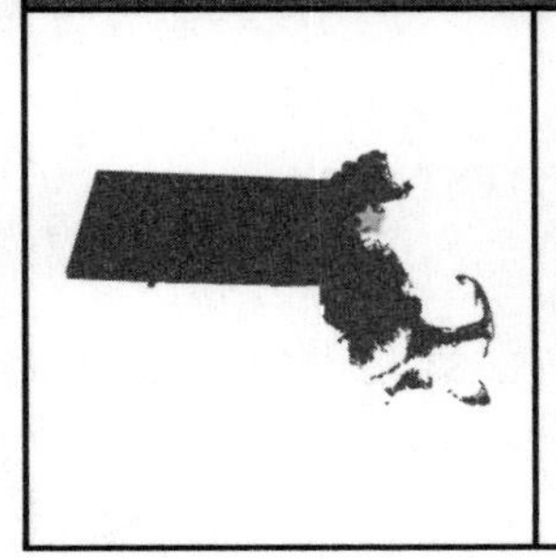

LOST $10.3 billion

LOST 76,147 people

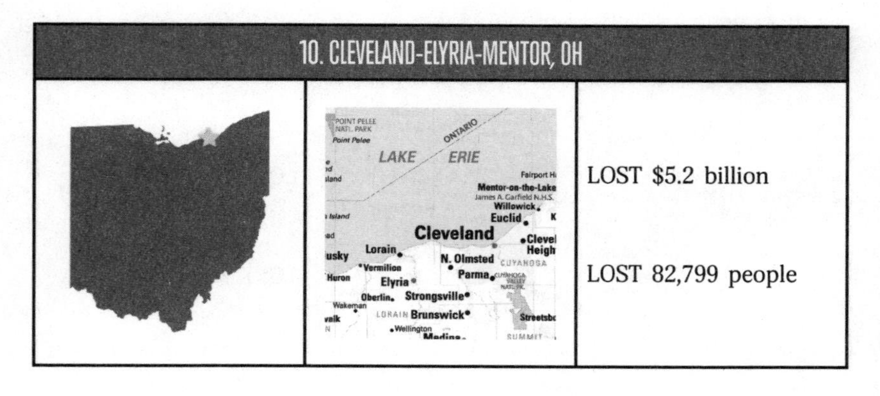

Total loss bottom 10: $186.8 billion

All told, the top 10 MSAs gained—again, solely through income migration—over $106 billion. That's the market value of eBay and Target combined.[7]

At the other end, it's even more staggering: the bottom five MSAs lost $186.7 billion, or enough to fund the State Department of the United States for almost four years.[8]

These are massive sums of money. Even broken down to yearly levels, it represents tens of billions of dollars moving into and out of states every year. Remarkable. And it's a lot to take in, I know.

Let's take a closer look where we can really see the impact—in the individual MSAs. We'll start with the state that gained the most and whose MSAs, in turn, also benefited—the Sunshine State, Florida.

Scan here for supplemental and additional material, illustrations, video, and other information.

Chapter Three Endnotes:

[1] Elizabeth Malm and Gerald Prante, "Annual State-Local Tax Burden Ranking," Background Paper No. 65 (October 2012), the Tax Foundation, http://www.taxfoundation.org/sites/taxfoundation.org/files/docs/BP65_2010_Burdens_Report.pdf.

[2] Merck market value as of October 2012, Forbes.com.

[3] Verizon market value as of October 2012, Forbes.com.

[4] Google's 2011 revenue, Google, http://investor.google.com/financial/tables.html.

[5] Nike market value as of October 2012, Forbes.com.

[6] MSAs are composed of counties; to calculate the AGI coming into or out of an MSA we took the AGI figures for each of the counties in a particular MSA and added them. MSA populations, the U.S. Census Bureau, "Statistical Abstract of the United States: 2012, Table 20: Large Metropolitan Statistical Areas–Population: 1990 to 2010."

[7] Target and eBay market values as of October 2012, Forbes.com.

[8] State Department budget, http://www.whitehouse.gov/sites/default/files/omb/budget/fy2013/assets/state.pdf.

Note: Though the movement of working wealth may not be widely discussed (yet), there are many who share the views in this book: namely, that income moves to where it is most welcome tax-wise and that this has a profound effect on state and local economies. Preceding each of the next chapters, where we drill down to the local levels of income movement, is *A Personal Perspective,* an introductory missive from a commentator who lives or works in that region and offers his views of income migration and the impact of taxes and movement on their local economy.

Chapter Four

A Personal Perspective

A WARM WELCOME FROM THE SUNSHINE STATE

By Joseph Calhoun

I was watching the Miami Heat play the New York Knicks on TV recently. Unfortunately for this Miami fan, the game was out of hand by the fourth quarter, with the Knicks pulling away for their second 20-plus point victory over Miami's champion Heat this season. Late in the game, a chant started up in the crowd: "Let's go New York! Let's go New York!"

There are two strange things about that.

First, Knicks fans, at least in the last few seasons, haven't often had any reason to be cheering in the

fourth quarter of a game against the Heat. Second, the game was being played at the American Airlines Arena—*in Miami.*

My parents moved to Miami in the late 1970s, way back before Miami Beach was transformed into the Art-Basel-hosting, $15-cocktail-swilling paradise destination for the International Jet Set Nouveaux Riche that it is now. Back then Miami was still mostly just a retirement haven from the cold winters up north and a place for Cuban exiles to await the demise of Fidel Castro. Miami Beach was a sleepy town of retirees who enjoyed the sun, the golf, a low cost of living, and, as an added bonus, no state income tax. They might have first come down to escape the cold but they came back and stayed to escape the high taxes. And they keep coming. Not to Miami Beach so much anymore—Wolfie's is closed—but New York and New Jersey keep raising taxes and the Jets, Mets, Yankees, Giants, and the much-despised Knicks fans keep coming. They might not like the taxes up north, but their sports team loyalties appear eternal.

The wonderful thing about making Florida your home is not only is there no income tax, but we also generate a lot of our tax revenue from out-of-state citizens and other foreigners who make

tourism the top industry in the Sunshine State. That has kept property taxes, at least until the last housing boom, low compared to other states. Total sales taxes average about 7 percent and the rest consists of a hodgepodge of taxes that are primarily paid by tourists who don't get to vote on such matters. The corporate income tax is just 5 percent. The result is a dynamic economy that is now less dependent on tourism and construction, the two primary drivers of the economy since Henry Flagler built his railroad. Florida is now the fourth largest exporter in the U.S. and seems likely to keep growing with the changes to the Panama Canal. Financial services, particularly international banking, are also major contributors to state GDP.

Florida was from its beginning a state designed to attract new residents. Until air conditioning became widespread, quite frankly, we had no choice but to create a friendly tax environment. Yes, the winters are nice but if you've ever been through a power outage in August, you know it took a hardy soul to brave a Miami summer armed with nothing but a fan and mosquito repellant. So, the income tax is specifically prohibited by our state constitution and we do our best to keep the tax

burden low. That recipe has worked for a long time, and it is still working. We have periodic real estate booms—mostly in the odd- and even-numbered decades—but the busts never last long and newcomers always absorb the excess supply. Other than the periodic nationwide recession or oil platform explosion, the Florida economy grows pretty steadily with population growth.

As you'll find out in this chapter, Floridians are on the move, too. There aren't too many native Floridians, and native Miamians are even more rare, but I've been happily married to one for the last 26 years. As she puts it—usually when we're stuck in traffic—Miami would be a nice place to live again if a couple million people would just leave.

Unfortunately for her and other longtime residents, that isn't happening. The largest influx of new residents to Naples, a short drive across Alligator Alley, is actually from the Miami area. Floridians might move around, but all of them know a pay cut and an ice scraper await them in almost any other state. And once you've become accustomed to wearing shorts in January and answering "no" on TurboTax when it asks if you want to download your state income tax forms, well, it's

hard to just give that up.

So, if you're reading this to see where you might relocate to escape the tax man, come on down to Florida. In fact, come all the way down to South Florida and buy my house. 1950s construction—survived a direct hit from Hurricane Andrew—with central air. I'm thinking about moving to Naples.

~

Joseph Calhoun is the founder and CEO of Alhambra Investment Partners.

Chapter Four

THE SUNSHINE STATE

Florida flourishes like no other

Florida, as we have already discussed, enjoyed a massive influx of both income and people between 1995 and 2010. During that period, 905,856 people migrated to the Sunshine State, bringing with them $86.4 billion in aggregate income. Using our mapping of IRS data, we know exactly how many people moved, the states and counties they came from, and even the adjusted gross income (AGI) per person. Here are the top 10 *state* sources for people migrating to Florida and the total AGI they took with them:

1.	New York	$16.8 billion
2.	New Jersey	$10.2 billion
3.	Illinois	$6.2 billion
4.	Ohio	$5.9 billion
5.	Pennsylvania	$5.7 billion
6.	Michigan	$4.8 billion
7.	Massachusetts	$4.7 billion
8.	Connecticut	$4.3 billion
9.	Maryland	$3.7 billion
10.	Virginia	$2.9 billion

New York lost the most aggregate income. That state lost half a million people and nearly $17 billion to Florida over that 15-year period alone. (And that's just to Florida. All told, over that 15-year period, New York lost a whopping $58.6 billion and 771,736 people, which we will discuss in the next chapter.)

We can drill down even further, to the county level. Here are the top 10 counties (and MSAs) from which people moved to Florida and the total AGI they took with them:

1.	Cook County, IL (Chicago MSA)	$3.2 billion
2.	Suffolk County, NY (NY MSA)	$2.9 billion
3.	Nassau County, NY (NY MSA)	$2.8 billion
4.	Fairfield County, CT (Bridgeport MSA)	$2.4 billion
5.	Queens County, NY (NY MSA)	$2.3 billion
6.	New York County, NY (NY MSA)	$1.8 billion
7.	Bergen County, NJ (NY MSA)	$1.8 billion
8.	Westchester County, NY (NY MSA)	$1.7 billion
9.	Oakland County, MI (Detroit MSA)	$1.6 billion
10.	Kings County, NY (NY MSA)	$1.4 billion

Again, we see a massive migration from New York. Of those 10 counties, 7 are in the NY MSA, totaling $12.9 billion in this list alone.

Why? Why is Florida so attractive (and not just to New Yorkers)? Well, as we know, Florida has lovely beaches and wonderful weather. There aren't that many places in the United States where you can enjoy a 70-degree day in January. But the state of Florida also has no state personal income tax and a mid-range state-local tax burden per capita.

It's no surprise then that 5 of the 10 MSAs in the country that gained the most aggregate income between 1995 and 2010 are in Florida:

- Miami-Fort Lauderdale-Pompano Beach: gained $11.9 billion
- Naples-Marco Island: gained $10.1 billion
- Tampa-St. Petersburg-Clearwater: gained $9.8 billion
- Cape Coral-Fort Myers: gained $9 billion
- North Port-Bradenton-Sarasota: gained $8.8 billion

Those five MSAs alone gained $49.5 billion. That's enough to buy the Miami Dolphins 49 times over.[1] And from our mapping of IRS data, we can see exactly where the money came from and where it went in Florida. Let's start in Miami.

MIAMI-FORT LAUDERDALE-POMPANO BEACH

According to the U.S. Census Bureau, the Miami-Fort Lauderdale-Pompano Beach MSA (which I will simply refer to as the Miami MSA from here on) is the eighth largest in the United States, with 5,565,000 people, as of the 2010 census. That's up more than 37 percent—or 1.5 million people—from its 1990 population of 4,056,000. The Miami MSA encompasses three counties: Broward County, Miami-Dade County, and Palm Beach County.

Clearly, the area is one of the most popular in the country, featuring as it does fantastic weather, dynamic culture, and great beaches and activities. The Miami area is geographically blessed and is a mecca for many people, for many reasons. Great weather? Check. Access to the ocean? Check. Vibrant culture? Check. Check. Check.

Given all it has going for it, one might be hard-pressed to need other reasons to move to the Miami area. But, as we know, Florida also has no state personal income tax and a fairly low per capita state-local tax burden that falls in the middle of the country (the Tax Foundation ranks Florida 27 out of 50). Add these tax facts in and you just might have a perfect storm for encouraging income migration. It certainly did the trick for the tens of thousands of people who moved into the Miami MSA from outside the state of Florida, bringing with them $11.9 billion in aggregate income. Again, it must be remembered that the $11.9 billion that came specifically into the Miami MSA does *not* reflect income derived from working in the state of Florida; this is income that *moved* to Florida, and specifically into that MSA. This is aggregate income that came to the Miami MSA from other states and counties.

Which other states and counties? We know that too, from the same source: the IRS Division of Statistics. Here are the top 10 counties, by population, from which people migrated to the Miami MSA between 1995 and 2010:

	County	Migrants
1.	Queens County, NY (NY MSA)	20,559
2.	Nassau County, NY (NY MSA)	17,802
3.	Kings County, NY (NY MSA)	14,659
4.	Suffolk County, NY (NY MSA)	11,942
5.	Bronx County, NY (NY MSA)	7,361
6.	Westchester County, NY (NY MSA)	6,799
7.	Bergen County, NJ (NY MSA)	6,409
8.	New York County, NY (NY MSA)	5,944
9.	Cook County, IL (Chicago MSA)	5,626
10.	Hudson County, NJ (NY MSA)	4,830

And here are the top 10 places by income migration:

1.	Nassau County, NY (NY MSA)	$1.48 billion
2.	New York County, NY (NY MSA)	$1.09 billion
3.	Queens County, NY (NY MSA)	$1.03 billion
4.	Suffolk County, NY (NY MSA)	$890 million
5.	Cook County, IL (Chicago MSA)	$800 million
6.	Bergen County, NJ (NY MSA)	$770 million
7.	Fairfield County, CT (Bridgeport MSA)	$690 million
8.	Westchester County, NY (NY MSA)	$660 million
9.	Kings County, NY (NY MSA)	$640 million
10.	Monmouth County NJ (NY MSA)	$440 million

Wow. New Yorkers love the Miami area. With the exception of Chicago and Bridgeport, every one of the top 10 counties is part of the New York MSA. In fact, with the exception of Chicago and Bridgeport, every one of the top *20* counties from which people and incomes moved to the Miami MSA is from the New York MSA. Of the $11.9 billion in aggregate income that migrated into the Miami MSA between 1995 and 2010, almost $11 billion came from the New York metropolitan area alone.

Why? How do we explain a migration of $11.9 billion from essentially one geographic area? How do we explain such a seismic shift? Maybe people flocked to the Miami area because of the weather. But maybe people fled New York because it has the highest state-local tax burden in the country: 12.3 percent, according to the Tax Foundation. New York has a top state personal income tax rate of 8.82 percent (cut in 2012 from 8.97 percent) and a state per capita tax burden of $6,375. Add to that the extraordinarily high New York City taxes (up to 3.876 percent, on top of state taxes) and you might have a recipe for some seriously high taxes. No wonder people are moving. If I were the governor of New York or New Jersey, or the mayor of any city in New York's MSA, I might take notice of this.

But Miami is not the only place New Yorkers migrated. They like the Gulf side, too.

NAPLES-MARCO ISLAND

The Naples MSA is tiny compared with Miami. According to the U.S. Census Bureau, the Naples-Marco Island MSA has a population of 322,000 people, as of the 2010 census. The population more than doubled between 1990 and 2010. The Naples MSA encompasses just one county, Collier County, but what a county it is.

The Naples MSA/Collier County has two distinct identities. One the one hand, much of it is composed of huge tracts of the undeveloped Florida Everglades. On the other hand, you have the gorgeous Gulf Coast, which tourism officials call the Paradise Coast, and with good reason. Located on the warm shores of the Gulf, the coastal areas boast beautiful white sandy beaches, moderate water temperatures, and some excellent fishing. Naples-Marco Island is a haven for vacationers, retirees, and fishermen. For many, it's paradise.

The cumulative 31,745 people who moved there between 1995 and 2010, bringing $10.1 billion in aggregate income with them, might agree. Roughly $671 million in aggregate income moved into Collier County every year over that period. That's a pretty impressive amount of money for a small county with only 322,000 people. The question is, why?

Well, obvious reasons are the idyllic location and the favorable tax situation in Florida. No state personal income taxes and a mid-range per capita state tax burden mean that people get to keep more of their money, and do so in an enviable climate. If you are looking for low taxes and a beautiful setting, you can't do much better than the Naples MSA. And clearly, thousands of people agreed, to the tune of $10 billion.

When you have an influx of people and money that large, it helps to examine where all that AGI came from. So let's take a closer look. Here are the top 10 places, by population, from which people moved to the Naples MSA between 1995 and 2010:

1.	Miami-Dade County, FL (Miami MSA)	2,825
2.	Cook County, IL (Chicago MSA)	1,828
3.	Broward County, FL, (Miami MSA)	1,604
4.	Suffolk County, NY (NY MSA)	1,153
5.	Middlesex County, MA (Boston MSA)	929
6.	Oakland County, MI (Detroit MSA)	903
7.	Fairfield County, CT (Bridgeport MSA)	888
8.	Nassau County, NY (NY MSA)	824
9.	Cuyahoga County, OH (Cleveland MSA)	763
10.	Essex County, MA (Boston MSA)	744

It's interesting that, unlike with the Miami MSA, here there is no single place from which people overwhelmingly moved, as they did from the New York area to Miami. Instead, for

Naples, we see a smattering of places from which people came—Miami, Chicago, New York, Boston, Cleveland, and Detroit. Each of those areas is geographically distinct, yet, with the exception of Florida and the Miami migrants, each has a commonality: high state personal income taxes or high per capita state-local tax burdens.

Let's take a closer look at those states (again, tax burden rankings and rates are from the Tax Foundation):

- New York State has a top personal income tax rate of 8.82 percent and the highest state-local tax burden in the country.
- The state of Illinois has a top income tax rate of 5 percent (recently raised from 3 percent) and ranks 11th in the nation in state-local tax burdens.
- Ohio has a top state income tax rate of 5.93 percent and ranks 20th in state-local tax burdens.
- Massachusetts has a top income tax rate of 5.3 percent and has the eighth highest state-local tax burden in the country.

Again, Florida has zero personal income taxes and ranks 27th in the nation in per capita state tax burdens.

So that's where the most people came from. Now let's look at where the most income came from. Here are the top 10 counties from which *income* moved:

1.	Hennepin County, MN (Minneapolis MSA)	$440 million
2.	Cook County, IL (Chicago MSA)	$390 million
3.	St. Louis County, MO (St. Louis MSA)	$270 million
4.	Oakland County, MI (Detroit MSA)	$240 million
5.	Allegheny County, PA (Pittsburg MSA)	$230 million
6.	Fairfield County, CT (Bridgeport MSA)	$200 million

7.	Lake County, IL (Chicago MSA)	$190 million
8.	Cuyahoga County, OH (Cleveland MSA)	$160 million
9.	Bergen County, NJ (NY MSA)	$150 million
10.	Westchester County, NY (NY MSA)	$150 million

The movement of income is fairly widely disbursed and the totals more broadly spread out, but here we see some new entrants: Minnesota, Missouri, Michigan, and Pennsylvania. How do their taxes stack up? Let's take a look:

MINNESOTA TAX FACTS
Top personal income tax rate: 7.85%
State-local tax burden: 10.8% Taxes paid per capita: $4,727 Rank: 7
1995-2010 population lost: 4,860
AGI lost to other states: $4.1 billion (mostly to Florida)

MISSOURI TAX FACTS
Top personal income tax rate: 6%
State-local tax burden: 9% Taxes paid per capita: $3,328 Rank: 34
1995-2010 population lost: 40,959
AGI lost to other states: $1.6 billion (mostly to Florida)

MICHIGAN TAX FACTS	
	Top personal income tax rate: 4.35%
	State-local tax burden: 9.8% Taxes paid per capita: $3,503 Rank: 18
	1995-2010 population lost: 274,878
	AGI lost to other states: $15.6 billion (mostly to Florida)

PENNSYLVANIA TAX FACTS	
	Top personal income tax rate: 3.07%
	State-local tax burden: 10.2% Taxes paid per capita: $4,183 Rank: 10
	1995-2010 population lost: 123,072
	AGI lost to other states: $6.9 billion (mostly to Florida)

Again, we see the same pattern: people and their incomes moved from states with higher personal and state per capita tax burdens to Florida, a state with no personal income taxes and a mid-range per capita state tax burden. Is this definitive proof that money (in this case, personal income) moves to where it is most welcome–in other words to where it won't be heavily taxed? The evidence may not be definitive, but it sure is compelling.

Let's look at another of Florida's MSAs, Tampa-St. Petersburg-Clearwater.

TAMPA-ST. PETERSBURG-CLEARWATER

The Tampa-St. Petersburg-Clearwater MSA (Tampa MSA) is the 19th largest in the country, with about 2.8 million people, according to the Census Bureau. The Tampa MSA grew by more than 700,000 people from 1990 to 2010. It's a sprawling MSA, covering over 2,500 square miles and four counties: Hernando, Hillsborough, Pasco, and Pinellas.

Tampa is second only to Miami as Florida's most thriving and important commercial center. The Tampa MSA is home to a rich and vibrant arts, sports, and entertainment culture and is a popular destination for tourists, conventions, and athletes alike. For baseball fans, Tampa is a popular destination, as at least 10 Major League Baseball teams, as well as countless collegiate squads, hold their spring training in the area.

This thriving MSA enjoyed a gain of $9.8 billion in aggregate income between 1995 and 2010. Where did it come from? Here are the top 10 places from which that money moved:

1. Cook County, IL (Chicago MSA) $430 million
2. Suffolk County, NY (NY MSA) $430 million
3. Nassau County, NY (NY MSA) $290 million
4. Queens County, NY (NY MSA) $270 million
5. Broward County, FL (Miami MSA) $230 million
6. Fairfax County, VA (DC MSA) $190 million
7. Kings County, NY (NY MSA) $180 million
8. Miami-Dade County, FL (Miami MSA) $170 million
9. Fairfield County, CT (Bridgeport MSA) $160 million
10. DuPage County, IL (Chicago MSA) $160 million

Once again, we see New York leading the pack, with the New York MSA appearing four times in the top 10. Let's look at where the people came from. Here are the top 10 counties from which the most people moved:

1. Suffolk County, NY (NY MSA) 9,049
2. Queens County, NY (NY MSA) 6,494
3. Cook County, IL (Chicago MSA) 6,374
4. Broward County, FL (Miami MSA) 5,536
5. Nassau County, NY (NY MSA) 5,457
6. Miami-Dade County, FL (Miami MSA) 4,674
7. Kings County, NY (NY MSA) 4,391
8. Bronx County, NY (NY MSA) 3,451
9. Erie County, NY (Buffalo MSA) 3,260
10. Fairfield County, CT (Bridgeport MSA) 2,701

Again, the lion's share of people came from New York and specifically the New York City metropolitan area.

Let's check out another Florida MSA, Cape Coral-Fort Myers.

CAPE CORAL-FORT MYERS

Compared with Miami or Tampa, the Cape Coral-Fort Myers MSA is tiny, encompassing just one county, Lee, and 619,000 people, making it about twice the size of the Naples MSA. The Cape Coral-Fort Myers MSA nearly doubled in size from 1990 to 2010, adding 284,000 people.

Cape Coral-Fort Myers is a gorgeous area, covering about 1,200 square miles and sitting snugly on the Gulf, just above Naples. As such, it enjoys the same geographic benefits as Naples: warm Gulf waters, nice tropical weather, and beautiful beaches.

And, like its Naples neighbor, the Cape Coral MSA also enjoyed a stunning income migration: $9 billion between 1995 and 2010.

Here's where it came from:

1.	Cook County, IL (Chicago MSA)	$310 million
2.	Hamilton County, OH (Cleveland MSA)	$260 million
3.	Hennepin County, MN (Minneapolis MSA)	$220 million
4.	Fairfield County, CT (Bridgeport MSA)	$220 million
5.	St. Louis County, MO (St. Louis MSA)	$210 million

6.	Miami-Dade County, FL (Miami MSA)	$200 million
7.	Suffolk County, NY (NY MSA)	$180 million
8.	Broward County, FL (Miami MSA)	$180 million
9.	Oakland County, MI (Detroit MSA)	$180 million
10.	Lake County, IL (Chicago MSA)	$130 million

Similar to the Naples MSA, the income pattern here is more diverse, with income migrating from inside Florida, as well as from Chicago, Cleveland, Detroit, St. Louis, Minneapolis, and New York. Let's look at where the people came from:

1.	Collier County, FL (Naples MSA)	7,931
2.	Miami-Dade County, FL (Miami MSA)	6,874
3.	Broward County, FL (Miami MSA)	4,172
4.	Cook County, IL (Chicago MSA)	2,605
5.	Suffolk County, NY (NY MSA)	2,106
6.	Oakland County, MI (Detroit MSA)	1,344
7.	Nassau County, NY (NY MSA)	1,323
8.	Queens County, NY (NY MSA)	1,170
9.	Cuyahoga County, OH (Cleveland MSA)	1,138
10.	Wayne County, MI (Detroit MSA)	1,075

Again, we see a similar pattern: lots of people from inside the state plus New York and many from the Midwest. Now let's look at the last Florida MSA, North Port-Bradenton-Sarasota.

NORTH PORT-BRADENTON-SARASOTA

The North Port-Bradenton-Sarasota MSA sits just below the Tampa MSA on the Gulf side. It covers two counties, Manatee and Sarasota, about 2,000 square miles, and has a 2010 population of about 702,000 (up 213,000 from 1990).

It, too, gained a massive amount of AGI—$8.8 billion between 1995 and 2010.

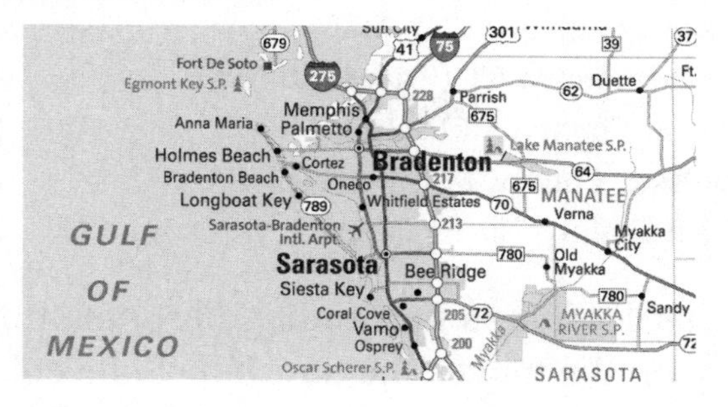

Here's where it came from:

1.	Cook County, IL (Chicago MSA)	$270 million
2.	Oakland County, MI (Detroit MSA)	$230 million
3.	Pinellas County, FL (Tampa MSA)	$220 million
4.	Fairfield County, CT (Bridgeport MSA)	$190 million
5.	Westchester County, NY (NY MSA)	$170 million
6.	Morris County, NJ (NY MSA)	$160 million
7.	Fairfax County, VA (DC MSA)	$160 million
8.	Suffolk County, NY (NY MSA)	$140 million
9.	Bergen County, NJ (NY MSA)	$140 million
10.	St. Louis County, MO (St. Louis MSA)	$140 million

Here, again, we see a lot of income coming from New York. Four of the top 10 counties from which income moved are in New York, specifically the New York MSA. In fact, more income migrated from the counties within the New York MSA than from any other counties or MSAs in the country.

Now let's look at the population migration:

1.	Charlotte County, FL (Port Charlotte MSA)	2,430
2.	Cook County, IL (Chicago MSA)	2,430
3.	Pinellas County, FL (Tampa MSA)	2,167

4.	Suffolk County, NY (NY MSA)	1,961
5.	Broward County, FL (Miami MSA)	1,701
6.	Nassau County, NY (NY MSA)	1,544
7.	Fairfield County, CT (Bridgeport MSA)	1,444
8.	Oakland County, MI (Detroit MSA)	1,278
9.	Middlesex County, MA (Boston MSA)	1,262
10.	Bergen County, NJ (NY MSA)	1,236

It's clear that Florida is the leading destination for people and money on the move. The Sunshine State enjoyed a net influx of $86.4 billion in AGI from 1995 to 2010. And Florida is also the number one destination for domestic migration: from 2000 to 2010, Florida enjoyed a cumulative population migration of 905,856. Florida is doing very well.

Rich States, Poor States: ALEC-Laffer State Economic Competitiveness Index, by Art Laffer, Stephen Moore, and Jonathan Williams, published every year by the American Legislative Exchange Council (ALEC), provides economic competitiveness and economic outlook rankings for all 50 states (1 being the best and 50 being the worst), using 15 different state policy variables, including top marginal personal income taxes, corporate taxes, property tax burdens, per capita burdens, minimum wage rates, and 10 other variables.

In the newest edition, *Rich States, Poor States* gave Florida an economic performance ranking of 13 and an economic outlook ranking of 13.[2] Pretty rosy, but it's easy to see why: Florida has no personal income taxes, a relatively low state tax burden (27th in the nation according to the Tax Foundation), low corporate income taxes, great weather, and vibrant culture. A great place to live. No wonder so many people are moving there.

Since so many people and the bulk of Florida's $86.4 billion net gain in AGI came from the New York area, let's go up there and take a closer look at the Empire State and its crown jewel, the Big Apple.

Scan here for supplemental and additional material, illustrations, video, and other information.

Chapter Four Endnotes:

[1] Team valuation from "The Business of Football," Forbes.com, http://www.forbes.com/nfl-valuations/list/.

[2] Arthur B. Laffer, Stephen Moore, Jonathan Williams, *Rich States, Poor States: ALEC-Laffer State Economic Competitiveness Index*, fifth edition (Washington, DC: American Legislative Exchange Council, 2012), http://www.alec.org/docs/RSPS_5th_Edition.pdf.

Chapter Five

A Personal Perspective

NEW YORK STATE: THE EMPIRE OF THE DEPARTED

By Deroy Murdock

"Start spreading the news. I'm leaving today..."

So begins "New York, New York," a song that Frank Sinatra made world famous. Alas, these days, rather than leaving *for* New York, thousands of people are leaving it behind.

As Travis H. Brown details in the following pages, New York State has been losing residents for years. While New York City's bright lights and endless excitement still lure people, Gotham has also seen many of its denizens rush the exits. While the

state's high cost of living and governmental hostility to businesses repel potential residents, a painful tax burden has led too many New Yorkers to cry "Uncle!" just before they recruit the moving vans.

"I have identified the most compelling incentive of all: a major tax break immediately available to all New Yorkers," Paychex, Inc. chairman Tom Golisano explained in a *New York Post* op-ed.[1] "To be eligible, you need do only one thing: move out of New York State." Golisano explained that he spent about 90 minutes transferring his voter registration, driver's license, and domicile certificate from New York to Florida. "Combined with spending 184 days a year outside New York, these simple procedures will save me over $5 million in New York taxes annually," Golisano calculated. "By domiciling in Florida, which has no personal income tax, I will save $13,800 every day. That's a pretty strong incentive."

"I left New York in 1997 strictly to get away from the onerous taxation," Rush Limbaugh declared on his national radio program, soon after Golisano spoke up.[2] "I don't want to talk numbers, but it was humongous....So I used my mobility and I moved." Limbaugh also decamped for income-tax-free Florida. Unfortunately for the popular broadcaster,

every day that he works in New York State (which he sometimes visits), the authorities tax a prorated portion of his income. They do so despite Limbaugh's protests and ongoing legal challenges. "My number is $20,000 a day, every day I work in New York, $20,000 a day," Limbaugh noted. "Sometimes 18, sometimes 20. My income changes year to year, so I guess it averaged out to $18,000 a day."

One-way traffic from the Empire State to the Sunshine State is so steady that Maplewood, New Jersey-based Harrington Moving and Storage specializes in easing that exodus. "Our professionals work hard to ensure that you don't have to during your move from New York to Florida," boasts the company's Web site. "You can rest assured knowing that your New York to Florida move will be smooth, relaxing, and seamless throughout."[3]

Contiguous to the Empire State, Connecticut is still smarting over the relocation of hedge-fund manager Edward Lampert. With an estimated net worth of $3 billion, according to *Forbes*, Lampert was considered the fifth wealthiest man in the Nutmeg State. In August 2011, Connecticut increased taxes by $875 million, retroactively to that January. It cut the maximum property-tax credit from $500 to

$300 and lifted its top state income tax rate from 6.5 percent to 6.7 percent. Then, on June 1, 2012, Lampert moved his company, ESL Investments, to Florida. Lampert also took with him the $10.6 billion that ESL reportedly controlled at that time.

"We are all aware that the changes to the tax structure in Connecticut last year have given many people pause as to whether this is the best place to do business and reside," Greenwich First Selectman Peter Tesei told the *Hartford Courant*. "I am concerned about the departure of Mr. Lampert and his firm, and would ask the state of Connecticut to take another look at its policies."[4]

Supply-side economists Arthur Laffer and Stephen Moore found similar unintended consequences just across the Hudson from New York. In 2004, New Jersey boosted its top tax rate from 6.35 percent to 8.97 percent. As they wrote in the *Wall Street Journal*, "Examining data from a 2008 Princeton study on the New Jersey tax hike on the wealthy, we found that there were 4,000 missing half-millionaires in New Jersey after that tax took effect."[5] State deficits soon erupted like Jersey barriers beside a ditch.

"Since many rich people also tend to be successful business owners, jobs leave with them or they never arrive in the first place," Laffer and Moore also pointed out. By definition, there is no way to measure, for instance, the positions that a retail chain does not create when it never opens stores in New York State because its owners prefer not to lose their shirts by crossing the George Washington Bridge into Manhattan.

For now, put aside the talent that New York State's high taxes scare off, the jobs and careers that they strangle in the crib, and the goods and services that New Yorkers cannot enjoy when the entrepreneurs who generate them vanish in disgust or simply stay out. The most pathetic aspect of Gotham's and the Empire State's punitive taxes is their counterproductivity. New York's sadistic tax code almost certainly chases away more revenues than government would collect if the state did not possess America's gold medal among per capita tax burdens—the highest in the country, according to the Tax Foundation.[6]

Referring to local liberal Democrats who hope to succeed him at City Hall and then jack up taxes on wealthy New Yorkers, Mayor Michael Bloomberg told journalists last October that this idea "is about as dumb a policy as I can think of....If you want to drive out the 1 percent of the people who pay roughly 50 percent of the taxes, or the 10 percent of the people who pay 70-odd percent of the taxes, that's as good a strategy as I know." Bloomberg added: "That's exactly the way to do it, and then our revenue would go away, and we wouldn't be able to have cops to keep us safe, firefighters to rescue us, or teachers to educate our kids."[7]

There's no avoiding this conclusion: regarding taxes, New York's state of mind is totally insane.

~

Deroy Murdock is a Fox News contributor, a nationally syndicated columnist with the Scripps Howard News Service, and a media fellow with the Hoover Institution on War, Revolution, and Peace at Stanford University. New York City's Neal K. Carter, Esq. furnished research for this piece.

Chapter Five Personal Perspective Endnotes:

[1] Tom Golisano, "Adios New York," *New York Post* (May 20, 2009), http://www.nypost.com/p/news/opinion/opedcol-

umnists/item_IlYA0ONr3hj3c31ZrkWCFJ;jsessionid=26D-96F89A5257206EB23D960F58B31C9.

[2] Rush Limbaugh, "My Advice for Tom Golisano," the Rush Limbaugh Show (May 20, 2009), http://www.rushlimbaugh.com/daily/2009/05/20/my_advice_for_thomas_golisano.

[3] Harrington Movers, http://www.harringtonmovers.com/services/moving/interstate/moving-from-ny-to-fl.php?rid=gaw-interstateny&gclid=CObL_OKq_LMCFYZM4Aod4F4AWQ.

[4] Dan Haar, "Exit of Hedge Fund Billionaire For Florida Raises Question: Who's Next?" *Hartford Courant* (June 7, 2012), http://articles.courant.com/2012-06-07/business/hc-hedge-fund-moves-florida-20120606_1_tax-revenue-fund-managers-personal-income.

[5] Arthur Laffer and Stephen Moore, "Soak the Rich, Lose the Rich," *Wall Street Journal* (May 18, 2009), http://online.wsj.com/article/SB124260067214828295.html.

[6] The Tax Foundation, http://taxfoundation.org/article/state-and-local-tax-burdens-all-states-one-year-1977-2010.

[7] Dana Rubinstein, "Taxing the rich is 'about as dumb a policy as I can think of,' Bloomberg says," *Capital New York* (Oct. 8, 2012), http://www.capitalnewyork.com/article/politics/2012/10/6537983/taxing-rich-about-dumb-policy-i-can-think-bloomberg-says.

Chapter Five

NEW YORK: THE EMPIRE STATE STRIKES OUT

A big bite out of the Big Apple

New York has a lot going for it. Not only is it home to the Big Apple, but it also boasts some of the most beautiful geography in the country—the Finger Lakes, the Adirondacks, the Catskills, Saratoga Springs, the Hamptons, and, of course, Niagara Falls.

Though Albany is the state capital, it is New York City that is widely recognized as the heart of the state. New York is a beacon in the worlds of finance and fashion, arts and entertainment, and more. It has long been a bastion of commerce and culture, capitalism and intellectual pursuit (both high and low). It is truly one of the greatest cities in the world.

It's also one of the largest. According to the Census Bureau, the population of New York City proper—which includes the boroughs of Manhattan, Brooklyn, the Bronx, Queens, and Staten Island—is 8,244,910, making it the largest city in the U.S.

The New York Metropolitan Statistical Area (NY MSA)–which covers 23 counties in three states–is also the most heavily populated in the country and the fourth most populated in the world, with 18,897,000 people, according to the Census Bureau. The New York MSA grew by two million people from 1990 to 2010, with the bulk of that growth taking place between 1990 and 2000.

But New York–the state, the MSA, and the city–is also first in another category, and it's not a good one. New York has seen billions of dollars in AGI move to other places. Sadly, New York is the poster child for income migration, and it's the state that lost the most AGI of any state in the country between 1995 and 2010: $58.6 billion.

Here are the numbers:

NEW YORK TAX FACTS	
	Top personal income tax rate: 8.82%
	State-local tax burden: 12.8% Taxes paid per capita: $6,375 Rank: 1 (highest in the country)
	1995-2010 population lost: 771,736
	AGI lost to other states: $58.6 billion

And here are some comparisons:

- The entire state of New York lost enough AGI–$58.6 billion–to build 39 Yankee Stadiums.[1]
- Averaged over 15 years, that's $3.9 billion a year, or $10.7

million a day that left the state.

- The NY MSA, which encompasses 23 counties in three states, saw $66.1 billion in AGI leave—that's more than twice the net worth of New York Mayor Michael Bloomberg.[2]
- The city of New York—just the five boroughs—saw a loss of $43.8 billion, about the market value of Time Warner, one of the city's commercial anchors.[3]

That's a big bite out of not just the Big Apple, but the whole state of New York. So let's start there.

THE STATE OF NEW YORK STATE

The state of New York saw a whopping net loss of $58.6 billion in AGI from 1995 to 2010. That's about 58 times Broadway's 2011-2012 revenue.[4] And 771,736 people moved away, too, which, according to the Census Bureau, is about the population of the city of Buffalo and the entire borough of Staten Island combined.

We know exactly where that income went. Here are the top 10 states that received New York's migrating AGI:

1.	Florida	$16.8 billion
2.	New Jersey	$11.6 billion
3.	Connecticut	$5.4 billion
4.	North Carolina	$4 billion
5.	California	$3.3 billion
6.	Pennsylvania	$2.9 billion
7.	Virginia	$2.1 billion
8.	Georgia	$2 billion
9.	South Carolina	$1.8 billion
10.	Texas	$1.6 billion

We can break it down by county. Here are the top 10 county destinations for New York State's AGI:

1.	Fairfield County, CT	$4.9 billion
2.	Palm Beach County, FL	$4.3 billion
3.	Monmouth County, NJ	$2.2 billion
4.	Bergen County, NJ	$2.2 billion
5.	Broward County, FL	$2.1 billion
6.	Middlesex County, NJ	$1.8 billion
7.	Essex County, NJ	$1.6 billion
8.	Maricopa County, AZ	$1.2 billion
9.	Hudson County, NJ	$1.2 billion
10.	Los Angeles County, CA	$1.1 billion

Let's look closer at the New York MSA and then the city of New York.

THE NEW YORK MSA

The New York Metropolitan Statistical Area (NY MSA)—as defined by the Census Bureau and officially called New York-Northern New Jersey-Long Island, NY, NJ, PA—is the biggest in the country, with 18,897,000 people in 23 counties in three states:

- Bergen County, NJ
- Bronx County, NY
- Essex County, NJ
- Hudson County, NJ
- Hunterdon County, NJ
- Kings County, NY
- Middlesex County, NJ
- Monmouth County, NJ

- Morris County, NJ
- Nassau County, NY
- New York County, NY
- Ocean County, NJ
- Passaic County, NJ
- Pike County, PA
- Putnam County, NY
- Queens County, NY
- Richmond County, NY
- Rockland County, NY
- Somerset County, NJ
- Suffolk County, NY
- Sussex County, NJ
- Union County, NJ
- Westchester County, NY

The New York MSA lost a staggering $66.1 billion dollars in AGI from 1995 to 2010. That's a tremendous amount of money–about enough to fund New York City for about a year, or New York State for about six months.[5]

Remember, MSAs can include counties outside of a state, so it is possible for an MSA to lose more than a particular state. In this case, the NY MSA includes counties in three states–New York, New Jersey, and Pennsylvania–which is why the New York MSA lost more than the state of New York.

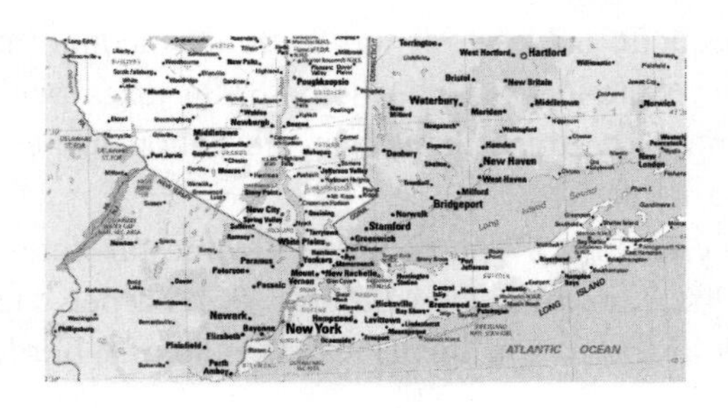

From our mapping of the IRS data, we can see exactly where the income went. Here are the top 10 destinations for the NY MSA's income:

1.	Palm Beach County, FL (Miami MSA)	$6.1 billion
2.	Fairfield County, CT (Bridgeport MSA)	$5.3 billion
3.	Broward County, FL (Miami MSA)	$2.6 billion
4.	Orange County, NY (Poughkeepsie MSA)	$2 billion
5.	Dutchess County, NY (Poughkeepsie MSA)	$1.5 billion
6.	Maricopa County, AZ (Phoenix MSA)	$1.5 billion
7.	Monroe County, PA (Stroudsburg MSA)	$1.4 billion
8.	Los Angeles County, CA (LA MSA)	$1.3 billion
9.	Lee County, FL (Fort Myers MSA)	$1.2 billion
10.	Mercer County, NJ (Trenton MSA)	$1.2 billion

Florida leads, with three MSAs receiving nearly $10 billion in AGI. But this is interesting: Florida is the only destination with zero personal income taxes. The others have varied tax rates. Again, tax burdens and rankings are from the Tax Foundation:

- Arizona: 4.54 percent personal income tax; 8.4 percent state-local tax burden; $3,006 taxes paid per capita, ranking it a low 40th in the nation in per capita state tax burdens.
- California: 13.3 percent top personal income tax rate; 11.2 percent state-local tax burden; $4,934 taxes paid per capita, ranking it the fourth highest in the nation in per capita state tax burdens.
- Connecticut: 6.7 percent top personal income tax rate; 12.3 percent state-local tax burden; $6,984 taxes paid per capita, ranking it the third highest in the nation in per capita state tax burdens.
- Pennsylvania: 3.07 percent top income tax rate; 10.2 percent state-local tax burden; $4,183 taxes paid per capita, ranking it 10th in the nation in per capita state tax burdens.

- New Jersey: 8.97 percent top personal income tax rate; 12.4 percent state-local tax burden; $6,689 taxes paid per capita, ranking it the second highest in the nation in per capita state tax burdens.

Income fled the New York MSA, but it didn't necessarily go far or to places with appreciably lower taxes (though six of the next 10 destinations were to Florida and Nevada, both states with zero income taxes, and every state has a lower per capita state tax burden).

And here is where the people went:

1.	Palm Beach County, FL (Miami MSA)	59,526
2.	Broward County, FL (Miami MSA)	53,010
3.	Fairfield County, CT (Bridgeport MSA)	30,680
4.	Orange County, NY (Poughkeepsie MSA)	30,095
5.	Orange County, FL (Orlando MSA)	26,186
6.	Monroe County, PA (Stroudsburg MSA)	25,141
7.	Maricopa County, AZ (Phoenix MSA)	21,409
8.	Dutchess County, NY (Poughkeepsie MSA)	21,320
9.	Hillsborough County, FL (Tampa MSA)	20,401
10.	Los Angeles County, CA (LA MSA)	19,140

Because of our extensive data mapping, we can also drill down to each and every one of the 23 counties in the New York MSA to see exactly how much income fled and where, specifically, it went. That's a little too exhaustive to provide here, but you can go to the Web site and see for yourself.

Now let's take a look at New York City proper, the five boroughs and counties that make up the Big Apple.

NEW YORK CITY

Each borough of New York City sits in its own county:

- Manhattan–New York County
- Brooklyn–Kings County
- Bronx–Bronx County
- Queens–Queens County
- Staten Island–Richmond County

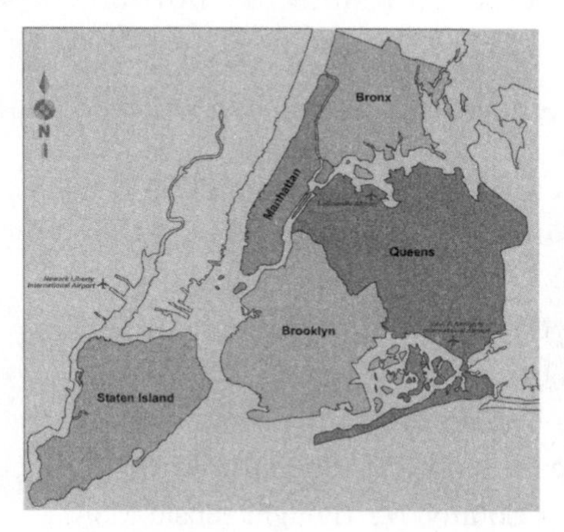

Here is how much AGI moved out of each of those five counties between 1995-2010:

- New York County (Manhattan): $11.5 billion moved out, $5.2 billion of which went out of the state.
- Kings County (Brooklyn): $11.3 billion moved out of the county, $6.5 billion out of the state.
- Bronx County (Bronx): $5.4 billion moved out of the county, $3.4 billion of which went out of the state.
- Queens County (Queens): $12.7 billion moved out of the county, $7.2 billion of which went out of the state.
- Richmond County (Staten Island): $2.9 billion moved out of the county, $1.2 billion out of the state.

The five boroughs of Manhattan saw enough AGI leave—$43.8 billion—to equal, roughly, the market value of all Major League Baseball, NBA, and NFL teams combined (with a little left over to give the refs a raise).[6] Brooklyn alone lost enough to build its brand-new billion-dollar Barclays Center 11 times over.

Staggering. These are massive amounts of money. Even reduced to annual levels they are stunning—every year, billions of dollars are leaving the city, the MSA, and the state of New York. How can New York let this happen?

I don't live in New York, but I find these figures shocking. If I were a New Yorker, either a denizen of the great city or the state, I would be pretty taken aback to see how much working wealth has left our area. And if I were the mayor of New York City, or the governor, or any elected local official I think I would take a long, hard look at these numbers and try to understand the correlation between my state and local tax policies and the massive migration of our working wealth. And then I think I would try very hard to do something about it.

And how did New York do on the 2012 ALEC-Laffer State Economic Competitiveness Index? With 1 being the best and 50 being the worst, New York was ranked 40th in economic performance and 50th—dead last in the country—in economic outlook. And New Jersey didn't fare much better: on the same scale, New Jersey ranked 45th in economic performance and 42nd in economic outlook.

But New York is not alone on the East Coast when it comes to huge losses in income. Though no other MSA or state in the country saw such massive losses, New York's neighbors didn't fare too well, either. Let's look at the other MSAs on the East Coast that also saw enormous amounts of working wealth move elsewhere: Boston, Philadelphia, and Washington, DC.

Scan here for supplemental and additional material, illustrations, video, and other information.

Chapter Five Endnotes:

[1] Mike Dodd, "Baseball's new palaces: Yankee Stadium and Mets' Citi Field, *USA Today* (April 6, 2009), http://usatoday30.usatoday.com/sports/baseball/2009-04-02-baseball-palaces_n.htm.

[2] Michael Bloomberg's net worth as of December 2012, http://www.forbes.com/profile/michael-bloomberg/.

[3] Time Warner market value as of October 2012, Forbes.com.

[4] David Ng, "Broadway posts record revenue, flat attendance for 2011-2012," *Los Angeles Times* (May 29, 2012), http://articles.latimes.com/2012/may/29/entertainment/la-et-cm-broadway-grosses-20120529.

[5] Budget of New York City, http://www.nyc.gov/html/omb/downloads/pdf/adopt12_expreso.pdf; budget of New York State, http://sunshinereview.org/index.php/New_York_state_budget.

[6] Team valuations from Forbes.com: "The Business of Baseball," http://www.forbes.com/mlb-valuations/list/; "The Business of Basketball," http://www.forbes.com/nba-valuations/list/; "The Business of Football," http://www.forbes.com/nfl-valuations/list/.

Chapter Six

A Personal Perspective

WAKE UP, EAST COAST POLITICIANS: TAXES ARE A *PRICE*

By John Tamny

Taxes are misnamed, and, partially because they are, the East Coast is suffering an economy-sapping outflow of some of its most productive citizens. The word "taxes" obscures the real impact of rates charged on income.

With the above in mind, it would be better to always and everywhere refer to taxes as "prices." Prices provide clarity where taxes apparently do not. Rather than saying that "the tax rate levied on the incomes of top earners in New York State is 8.82 percent," it would be clearer (and more accurate) to say, "top

earners are charged 8.82 percent for the right to live and work in the state of New York."

Once taxes are properly described as a price, voters will hopefully see how destructive they can be from a growth perspective. When we raise taxes on top earners, we increase the cost for them to live among us, transact with us, and to create businesses that employ us.

New Yorkers, and in particular citizens of Manhattan, might argue that tax rates don't matter, that the business, cultural, and lifestyle advantages to living in New York make the taxes levied for doing so irrelevant. That would have been a fair response, in 1975.

Certainly in 1975 a young equity trader, artist, or writer might have felt compelled to live where "those with talent" go to take "the final test," as writer Ken Auletta wrote in *The Streets Were Paved with Gold*, his 1975 classic book about New York City's debt troubles. Though the city was hurtling toward bankruptcy at the time, high tax rates could perhaps be justified thanks to limited options outside New York in the 1970s.

Fast forward nearly 40 years, and geographical limitations have been eroded. Technology, as they say, is like acid when it comes to burning through inefficiencies and, for that matter, discomfort. Those advances have made living in the cosmopolitan cities that dot the East Coast less necessary.

From a lifestyle perspective, it used to be that living in traditionally low-tax southern states was too uncomfortable due to the humid summers that define life below the Mason-Dixon Line. But thanks to Willis Carrier's invention of the air conditioner (ironically in Buffalo, New York), the low-tax South's weather limitations have largely been erased.

Though Wall Street used to be where financing of all manner of ideas took place, increasingly it's just a symbol, thanks to communication and computer advances that allow an equity trader to set up shop and work from virtually anywhere. Put plainly, finance that partially emanated from Wall Street led to technological advances that made working on Wall Street—the place—less important.

Consider the writer who at one time needed to be at the center of media; now, computer and Inter-

net advances have truly given life to the popular phrase "death of distance." Today's writer can file a story that can quickly reach all four corners of the earth just as easily from Manhattan, Kansas, as from Manhattan, New York.

As for culture, the rise of Netflix, satellite television, and the Internet means that living off the grid no longer means that one is limited to off-the-grid entertainment. Nowadays one can enjoy much of the culture that originates in New York minus the cost of living in New York.

All of which brings us back to the nosebleed tax rates levied on New Yorkers and, more broadly, most East Coast residents. Put plainly, the tax rate schemes have not evolved alongside technology. Because they haven't, New York and its other eastern neighbors are increasingly too expensive to live in.

Thanks to innovations either financed or intellectually conceptualized on the East Coast, that same East Coast has been rendered less essential as a place to live. Tax rates have gone up in eastern states alongside advances that make living there much less important, and the result has been an outward migration of the best and brightest.

To reverse the talents and brain drain, it's necessary that politicians in New York and elsewhere lower the cost of living on the East Coast. Lower tax rates are a very good place to start.

~

John Tamny is the editor of Forbes Opinions *and the Web site RealClearMarkets.com.*

Chapter Six

EAST COAST BLUES

Historic losses for America's historic cities and states

New York is not the only state or MSA on the East Coast to see billions of dollars in adjusted gross income move to more welcoming areas. The Boston, Philadelphia, and Washington, DC, MSAs, as well as their attendant states and counties, have all seen staggering sums of AGI flee. Let's start at the top, with Boston and the state of Massachusetts.

MASSACHUSETTS AND THE BOSTON MSA

Massachusetts is inarguably one of the most historic states in the country. Heck, it's where it all began; it's where the Mayflower landed and where Plymouth Colony was established in 1630. The nation's oldest college, Harvard, was founded there in 1636. Much of the Revolutionary War was fought in the area. It's the birthplace of America.

It's also a geographically gorgeous state. The Berkshires in the west are stunning year-round. The eastern part of the state is blessed with some of the most beautiful coastal areas and islands in the country: Buzzard's Bay, Cape Cod, Martha's Vineyard, Nantucket, and more. The state also boasts great, historic cities, like Boston, Salem, Marblehead, and Gloucester.

The population of Massachusetts is about 6.6 million people. The population of Boston proper is about 625,000. The Boston MSA, of course, is far larger than that, with a population of about 4.5 million people, making it the 10th largest metropolitan statistical area in the nation.

The Boston MSA—officially called Boston-Cambridge-Quincy, MA-NH—covers 4,674 square miles and seven counties, including three in neighboring New Hampshire:

- Essex County, MA
- Middlesex County, MA
- Norfolk County, MA
- Plymouth County, MA
- Rockingham County, NH
- Strafford County, NH
- Suffolk County, MA

So how did this historic state and MSA fare in terms of income movement? Not great. Between 1995 and 2010, Massachusetts saw a net loss of $10.8 billion in AGI. That's about four times the entire FY (fiscal year) 2013 budget of Boston, and about a third of the state's total FY2013 budget.[1] That's a lot of money.

BOSTON-CAMBRIDGE-QUINCY, MA, NH
State lost $10.8 billion
State lost 98,869 people
MSA lost $10.3 billion
MSA lost 76,147 people

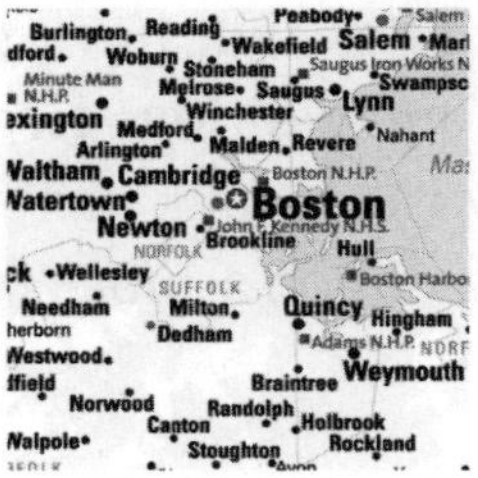

Where did it go? Here are the top five destinations by state:

1. Florida: gained $4.7 billion
2. New Hampshire: gained $2.9 billion
3. California: gained $1.4 billion
4. Maine: gained $806 million
5. North Carolina: gained $756 million

And, of course, we can break it down by county. Here are the top 10 destinations, by county and state, for the AGI leaving the state of Massachusetts:

1.	Rockingham County, NH	$1.6 billion
2.	Hillsborough County, NH	$1.2 billion
3.	Palm Beach County, FL	$809 million
4.	Collier County, FL	$631 million
5.	Lee County, FL	$465 million
6.	Maricopa County, AZ	$403 million
7.	York County, ME	$368 million
8.	San Diego County, CA	$356 million
9.	Sarasota County FL	$341 million
10.	Broward County, FL	$323 million

From this top 10 list, the two states that saw the biggest migration of Massachusetts's working wealth—a combined $5.4 billion—are also states that have no personal income tax: New Hampshire and Florida. Here is how all those states stack up, tax-wise (again, tax rates and rankings are from the Tax Foundation's most recent report):

Massachusetts

- Top state personal income tax rate: 5.3 percent
- State-local tax burden: 10.4 percent
- Taxes paid per capita: $5,422
- Rank: 8

New Hampshire

- Top state personal income tax rate: 0 percent
- State-local tax burden: 8.1 percent
- Taxes paid per capita: $3,717
- Rank: 44

Florida

- Top state personal income tax rate: 0 percent
- State-local tax burden: 9.3 percent
- Taxes paid per capita: $3,728
- Rank: 27

California

- Top state personal income tax rate: 13.3 percent
- State-local tax burden: 11.2 percent
- Taxes paid per capita: $4,934
- Rank: 4

Maine

- Top state personal income tax rate: 8.5 percent
- State-local tax burden: 10.3 percent
- Taxes paid per capita: $3,807
- Rank: 9

North Carolina

- Top state personal income tax rate: 7.75 percent
- State-local tax burden: 9.9 percent
- Taxes paid per capita: $3,535
- Rank: 17

So, about 100,000 people and $10.8 billion migrated out of the state. Why? Well, here is what we know: Massachusetts is a beautiful state, with tremendous geographic diversity, some of the best prep schools and universities in the world, great sports teams, and historic, vibrant cities. We also know that the state of Massachusetts has a top state personal income tax rate of 5.3 percent and a per capita state tax burden of $5,422, the eighth highest in the country. (Massachusetts is often dubbed "Taxachusetts.")

All told, the state of Massachusetts lost $10.8 billion in adjusted gross income between 1995 and 2010. Let's see how the Boston MSA—which again covers seven counties in Massachusetts and New Hampshire—fared.

As it turns out, the Boston MSA lost $10.3 billion between 1995 and 2010. That's about three times the market value of Boston's major professional sports teams—the Red Sox, Celtics, New England Patriots, and Boston Bruins—combined.[2]

Let's look a little closer at where that income went. Here are the top 10 counties and states to which the Boston MSA lost aggregate income:

1.	Worchester County, MA (Worchester MSA)	$1.5 billion
2.	Barnstable County, MA (Barnstable MSA)	$1.2 billion
3.	Hillsborough County, NH (Manchester MSA)	$1.1 billion
4.	Palm Beach County, FL (Miami MSA)	$670 million
5.	Bristol County, MA (Providence MSA)	$650 million
6.	Collier County, FL (Naples MSA)	$420 million
7.	York County, ME (Portland MSA)	$370 million
8.	Lee County, FL (Cape Coral MSA)	$360 million
9.	San Diego County, CA (San Diego MSA)	$310 million
10.	Maricopa County, AZ (Phoenix MSA)	$300 million

Of these destinations, about $3.4 billion stayed in the state of Massachusetts, $1.45 billion moved to Florida, $1.1 billion moved to New Hampshire, $370 million to Maine, $310 million to California, and $300 million to Arizona. That makes for an interesting migration pattern. Though some of the AGI that left the Boston MSA stayed in Massachusetts, the bulk of it, again, went to areas with lower taxes.

Let's leave the Commonwealth of Massachusetts and head down the coast to Philadelphia, another great and historic American city. How did Philly fare?

PENNSYLVANIA AND THE PHILLY MSA

The Keystone State is the sixth most populous state in the nation, with about 12.7 million people. Pennsylvania is known for both its history–if Boston is the birthplace of the nation, then Philly is certainly the cradle–and its industry. The state has seen its share of ups and downs, and this is evident when you take a look at the income migration pattern.

Though it wasn't hit nearly as hard as its northern neighbors, Pennsylvania saw a net loss of 123,000 people and $6.9 billion in AGI between 1995 and 2010. That's almost twice the market value of the Pittsburg Steelers, Philadelphia Eagles, Pittsburg Pirates, Philadelphia Phillies, and Philadelphia 76ers combined.[3]

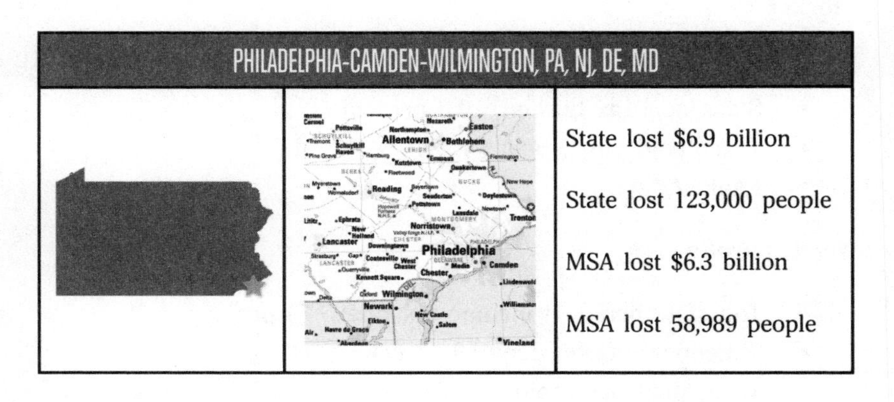

Here are the top five states to which that AGI moved between 1995 and 2010:

1. Florida: gained $5.7 billion
2. North Carolina: gained $1.6 billion
3. South Carolina: gained $970 million
4. California: gained $772 million
5. Virginia: gained $738 million

Let's look at the tax situation in Pennsylvania, and then at each of the five states above:

Pennsylvania

- Top state personal income tax rate: 3.07 percent
- State-local tax burden: 10.2 percent
- Taxes paid per capita: $4,183
- Rank: 10

So Pennsylvania is a fairly tax-heavy state. Now let's look at the states where the most AGI migrated:

Florida

- Top state personal income tax rate: 0 percent
- State-local tax burden: 10.3 percent
- Taxes paid per capita: $3,728
- Rank: 27

North Carolina

- Top state personal income tax rate: 7.75 percent
- State-local tax burden: 9.9 percent
- Taxes paid per capita: $3,535
- Rank: 17

South Carolina

- Top state personal income tax rate: 7 percent
- State-local tax burden: 8.4%
- Taxes paid per capita: $2,760
- Rank: 41

California

- Top state personal income tax rate: 13.3 percent
- State-local tax burden: 11.2 percent
- Taxes paid per capita: $4,934
- Rank: 4

Virginia

- Top state personal income tax rate: 5.75 percent
- State-local tax burden: 9.3 percent
- Taxes paid per capita: $4,336
- Rank: 30

Most of the AGI—some $8.7 billion—moved to where taxes were lower: Florida, North Carolina, and South Carolina.

Now let's look at the Philadelphia MSA.

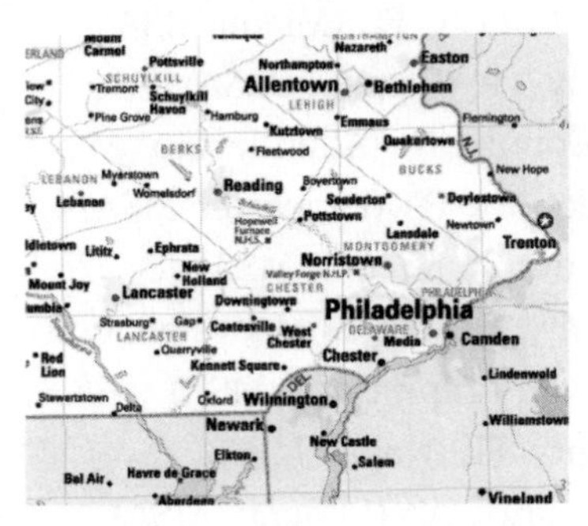

The Philadelphia MSA, officially known as Philadelphia–Camden–Wilmington, PA–NJ–DE–MD, is the fifth largest in the country, with nearly six million people. It's also geographically large, covering 5,118 square miles over 11 counties in 4 states:

- Bucks County, PA
- Burlington County, NJ

- Camden County, NJ
- Cecil County, MD
- Chester County, PA
- Delaware County, PA
- Gloucester County, NJ
- Montgomery County, PA
- New Castle County, DE
- Philadelphia County, PA
- Salem County, NJ

Between 1995 and 2010, the Philadelphia MSA lost $6.3 billion in AGI, almost twice the FY2013 budget of the city of Philadelphia.[4]

Where did it go? Here are the top 10 destinations for AGI leaving the Philadelphia MSA between 1995 and 2010:

1.	Palm Beach County, FL (Miami MSA)	$920 million
2.	Berks County, PA (Reading MSA)	$600 million
3.	Cape May County, NJ (Atlantic City MSA)	$440 million
4.	Lancaster County, PA (Lancaster MSA)	$380 million
5.	New York County, NY (NY MSA)	$370 million
6.	Sussex County, DE (no MSA designation)	$360 million
7.	Lee County, FL (Cape Coral MSA)	$340 million
8.	Collier County, FL (Napes MSA)	$330 million
9.	Maricopa County, AZ (Phoenix MSA)	$310 million
10.	Atlantic County, NJ (Atlantic City MSA)	$290 million

Again, Florida is the number one destination based on income migration. We already know the tax situation there, as well as in New York and Arizona, so let's look at Delaware and New Jersey:

Delaware

- Top state personal income tax rate: 6.75 percent
- State-local tax burden: 9.2 percent
- Taxes paid per capita: $3,728
- Rank: 31

New Jersey

- Top state personal income tax rate: 8.97 percent
- State-local tax burden: 12.4 percent
- Taxes paid per capita: $6,689
- Rank: 2

Why on earth would people move to a state with higher taxes? Well, in the case of New Jersey, Cape May is on the shore. It's a beautiful area. Taxes are not always the number one reason people move; however, as we've seen across the board, they appear to be a compelling one.

Let's end this chapter by looking at the nation's capital, Washington, DC.

THE DC MSA

Washington, DC is not just our nation's capital, it's also one of the most beautiful cities in the world and one of the most popular. Millions of tourists from all over the world flock to DC every year to see the monuments, memorials, and symbols of American freedom and democracy. Despite being a "company town," DC has a vibrant international culture and a sophisticated, cosmopolitan feel to it.

Washington, DC proper has a population of 617,996 people in just 61 square miles. The DC MSA, however, is much, much larger.

The DC MSA—formally known as Washington-Arlington-Alexandria, DC-VA-MD-WV—is the seventh largest in the country, with 5.7 million people. DC's MSA covers 5,564 square miles in three states, 21 counties, and the District of Columbia, which, of course, is not a state and has no county affiliation. (Despite the fact that DC is not a state, District residents pay federal taxes and so the IRS has taxpayer files on them.) Here are the 21 counties that comprise the DC MSA:

- Alexandria City, VA
- Arlington County, VA
- Calvert County, MD
- Charles County, MD
- Clarke County, VA
- District of Columbia
- Fairfax City, VA
- Fairfax County, VA
- Falls Church City, VA
- Fauquier County, VA
- Frederick County, MD

- Fredericksburg City, VA
- Jefferson County, WV
- Loudoun County, VA
- Manassas City, VA
- Manassas Park City, VA
- Montgomery County, MD
- Prince George's County, MD
- Prince William County, VA
- Spotsylvania County, VA
- Stafford County, VA
- Warren County, VA

How did DC do vis-à-vis income migration? Not well. Despite being the vibrant capital of the nation and one of the country's biggest MSAs, both the city proper and the MSA lost billions in AGI. Between 1995 and 2010, the city of Washington, DC saw a net population loss of 19,000 people and $3.4 billion in AGI. That's about twice the market value of the city's beloved Washington Redskins.[5]

The DC MSA fared even worse. Between 1995 and 2010, a cumulative 55,424 people actually moved into the MSA, but $11.3 billion in AGI moved out. That's about 20 percent more than the city of Washington, DC's FY2013 budget, and 10 times the annual budget of the area's massive Metro system.[6]

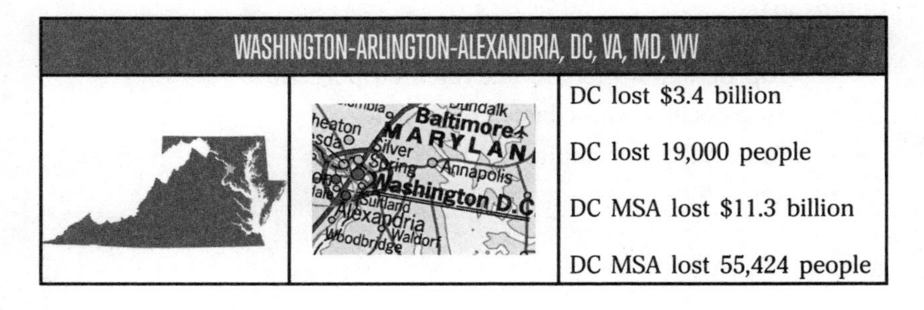

Eleven billion dollars is a tremendous amount of money. Why the migration? DC is a great, exciting place to live. But it's also an expensive one. Here are Washington, DC's tax facts:

District of Columbia

- Top personal income tax rate: 8.95 percent
- State-local tax burden: 9.3 percent
- Taxes paid per capita: $5,991
- Rank: DC is not a state, but the Tax Foundation would rank it 31st in the nation in per capita tax burdens.

Pretty high. So, where did that money go? Here are the top five places the AGI went to from the city of Washington, DC:

- Maryland: $2.4 billion; specifically Montgomery and Prince George's Counties
- Virginia: $727 million, specifically Arlington County, Fairfax County, and the city of Alexandria
- Florida: $266 million, specifically Miami-Dade and Palm Beach Counties
- California: $229 million, specifically Los Angeles and San Francisco Counties
- Colorado: $58 million, specifically Denver County

We know the tax facts for all of those states except Colorado:

Colorado

- Top personal income tax rate: 4.6 percent
- State-local tax burden: 9.1 percent
- Taxes paid per capita: $4,104
- Rank: 32

With the exception of California, all have lower personal income tax rates than DC, and all pay lower taxes per capita.

Let's look at the MSA. Where did that aggregate income go? Here are the top 10 counties to which the DC MSA's $11.3 billion migrated:

1. Anne Arundel County, MD (Baltimore MSA) $1.7 billion
2. Howard County, MD (Baltimore MSA) $890 million
3. Palm Beach County, FL (Miami MSA) $620 million
4. Washington County, MD (Hagerstown MSA) $520 million
5. Sussex County, DE (no MSA) $410 million
6. Berkeley County, WV (Hagerstown MSA) $390 million
7. Wake County, NC (Raleigh MSA) $370 million
8. Maricopa County, AZ (Phoenix MSA) $370 million
9. Frederick County, VA (Winchester MSA) $360 million
10. Culpepper County, VA (no MSA) $340 million

We don't know what the average per capita taxes are in the DC MSA—there are too many jurisdictions to calculate—but we know that a few of these destinations—namely Florida, Arizona, and West Virginia—have some of the lowest tax rates in the country. DC is a great city and great metropolitan area. But it's also one of the most expensive areas in the country. It's possible that $11 billion voted to move to more advantageous areas.

Let's take a trip across the country and see how the West Coast fared.

Scan here for supplemental and additional material, illustrations, video, and other information.

Chapter Six Endnotes:

[1] Boston's FY2013 budget, http://www.cityofboston.gov/news/default.aspx?id=5684; Budget of state of Massachusetts, Sunshinereview.org.

[2] Team market values from Forbes.com: "The Business of Baseball," http://www.forbes.com/mlb-valuations/list/; "The Business of Basketball," http://www.forbes.com/nba-valuations/list/; "The Business of Football," http://www.forbes.com/nfl-valuations/list/; and "The Business of Hockey," http://www.forbes.com/nhl-valuations/list/.

[3] Ibid.

[4] City of Philadelphia FY2013 budget, http://www.phila.gov/pdfs/Mayors_Operating_Budget_In_Brief_FY2013.pdf.

[5] "The Business of Football," http://www.forbes.com/nfl-valuations/list/.

[6] Washington, DC's FY2013 budget, http://cfo.dc.gov/sites/default/files/dc/sites/ocfo/publication/attachments/ocfo_fy2013_volume_1_executive_summary.pdf; Washington Metropolitan Area Transit Authority's FY2013 budget, http://www.wmata.com/about_metro/board_of_directors/board_docs/051012_3AFY2013Budget51012FAREVISED.pdf.

Chapter Seven

A Personal Perspective

CALIFORNIA'S LONG NIGHTMARE

By Thomas Del Beccaro

If you have traveled the world much at all, you know that simply mentioning that you are from California elicited pangs of jealousy. Until recently. Since California became a state, it has enjoyed steady and sometimes dramatic population and economic growth. Until recently. All in all, California was the land of unlimited promise and possibility. All of those things, until recently.

Over the last 15 years, California has changed dramatically. In the last redistricting, for a rare time in its 160-plus year history, California did not gain a

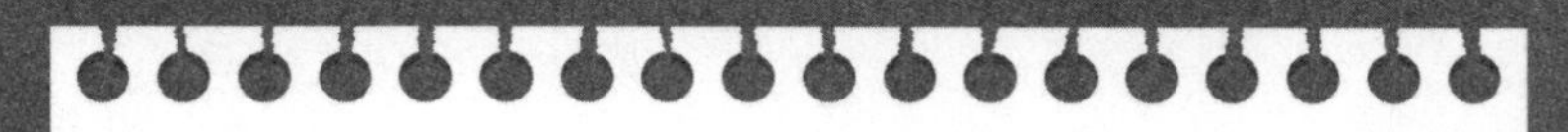

single congressional seat. In 1990, California gained seven House seats. In 2010, it gained none. Population growth has stopped. But there is more to the story.

According to famed Democratic demographer Joel Kotkin, "increasingly the only ones fit to survive in California are the very rich and those who rely on government spending....the state is run for the very rich, the very poor, and the public employees."[1] That is hardly an inviting sentiment for a state with underemployment topping 22 percent in 2012.

So how did the Golden State become so tarnished? Travis H. Brown's book holds the key.

Keep in mind that California has one of the most active state governments in the nation. Thousands of bills are considered each year by the very liberal legislature. Massive programs like universal health care pass committees with ease. Nearly 1,000 bills are signed each year.

Year after year those bills translate into staggering state debt. By some estimates, the state's pension deficit has surpassed $500 billion, more than five times the annual revenues of the state. Not to be

deterred, California's mercurial governor, Jerry Brown, is pushing a $100 billion high-speed rail system. What's a legislature to do in the face of all those bills, both legislative and monetary? Tax. Tax. Tax.

California, once the nation's leader in tax reform—a wave Ronald Reagan road to the White House—is now the national leader in tax burdens. Once the land of Prop 13, the legendary property tax reform that swept the nation, California now features this from its governor: After his November 2012 victory raising California's income taxes to the highest in the country, Jerry Brown answered "Yes, I do" to CNN's Candy Crowley's stark question: "Do you think California's the start of a tax-increase sweep?"[2]

Governor Brown's comment is the equivalent of a business owner walking out of his shop and loudly declaring to everyone on the street: "I have the highest prices on the block!" No rational business owner would do such a thing, but California's legislature and governor do just that.

As with many politicians, California's ruling party spends first and looks for money second. Invariably,

California has a shortfall. Indeed, for years, California's annual deficit was larger than the entire budget of more than 20 states.

Faced with those deficits, Democratic leaders simply take out their calculators. They believe that if you need more tax revenue you simply need to change the existing tax rate. By their logic, if you need to double the revenue, you simply need to double the tax rate. No business owner would use such logic in the face of poor sales revenues, but California Democrats do, and that is the heart of the problem.

California's Democratic leaders simply do not believe that ever-higher tax rates negatively affect the state economy. Year after year of unmet revenue projections don't give them pause. They simply don't believe that wealth reacts to changing tax laws, let alone moves out of state.

On that critical issue–how tax policy affects people's decisions, the economy, and state revenues–the sheer size of California is a glaring incubator of bad news. With Travis H. Brown's book, we finally have definitive data on just how bad the news is.

Thomas Del Beccaro is the chairman of the California Republican Party. He is the publisher of PoliticalVanguard.com, the author of The New Conservative Paradigm, *and a frequent talk radio and television commentator.*

Chapter Seven Personal Perspective Endnotes:

[1] Allysia Finley, "Joel Kotkin: The Great California Exodus," *Wall Street Journal* (April 20, 2012), http://online.wsj.com/article/SB10001424052702304444604577340531861056966.html.

2 Governor Jerry Brown on "State of the Union with Candy Crowley," CNN (November 12, 2012), www.cnn.com.

Chapter Seven

CALIFORNIA'S DREAMING

The Golden State's massive migration

California is America's Golden State. It's home to Hollywood, top universities, Silicon Valley, and great cities like San Francisco and Los Angeles. There, you'll find the Pacific Coast, Malibu, Big Sur, Carmel, and more. Just saying the names conjures beautiful beaches, golden sunshine, and the good life. California has it all: mountains, beaches, an ocean, movie stars, mansions, an eclectic international population, great universities, and world-class commerce, technology, and art.

California is the most populous state in the nation, with 37.7 million people, according to the Census Bureau. (It is also the third largest state in terms of area.) To be sure, California is a destination for a broad range of people—immigrants, computer scientists, innovators, surfers, aspiring actors, artists, and others.

But the IRS numbers tell a slightly different story. Between 1995 and 2010, this great state saw a net decline in population of 340,622 people and a loss of $31.8 billion in AGI, the most of any state except New York.

CALIFORNIA TAX FACTS	
	Top personal income tax rate: 13.3%
	State-local tax burden: 11.2% Taxes paid per capita: $4,934 Rank: 4
	Net loss of AGI: $31.8 billion

That is an extraordinary amount of aggregate income—$31.8 billion dollars. To give that some perspective, that's about 16 times times the market value of the most profitable animation studio in Hollywood, DreamWorks Animation SKG, which brought us *Shrek, Kung Fu Panda, Madagascar*, and other classics.[1]

Here are the top five states to which California lost AGI:

- Nevada, $8.2 billion
- Arizona, $6.3 billion
- Oregon, $4.9 billion
- Texas, $4.8 billion
- Washington, $3.9 billion

And here are the top 10 counties and states to which the most people and AGI went:

1.	Clark County, NV	$5.9 billion
2.	Maricopa County, AZ	$4.8 billion
3.	Washoe County, NV	$2.3 billion
4.	King County, WA	$1.4 billion
5.	Pima County, AZ	$1.1 billion
6.	Mohave County, AZ	$960 million
7.	Travis County, TX	$913 million
8.	Multnomah County, OR	$849 million
9.	Douglas County, NV	$814 million
10.	Yavapai County, AZ	$807 million

The bulk of the working wealth went to Nevada, which has no personal income taxes. Every state on that list has lower tax burdens (which include all taxes a citizen pays) than California. Here are the tax rates for the five states that enjoyed the bulk of California's AGI movement:

NEVADA TAX FACTS
Top personal income tax rate: 0%
State-local tax burden: 8.2% Taxes paid per capita: $3,297 Rank: 42
Net gain of AGI: $16 billion

ARIZONA TAX FACTS	
	Top personal income tax rate: 4.54%
	State-local tax burden: 8.4% Taxes paid per capita: $3,006 Rank: 40
	Net gain of AGI: $24.5 billion

OREGON TAX FACTS	
	Top personal income tax rate: 9.9%
	State-local tax burden: 10% Taxes paid per capita: $3,729 Rank: 16
	Net gain of AGI: $5.6 billion

TEXAS TAX FACTS	
	Top personal income tax rate: 0%
	State-local tax burden: 7.9% Taxes paid per capita: $3,104 Rank: 45
	Net gain of AGI: $22.1 billion

WASHINGTON TAX FACTS	
	Top personal income tax rate: 0%
	State-local tax burden: 9.3% Taxes paid per capita: $4,261 Rank: 28
	Net gain of AGI: $9.9 billion

Of those five states, three—Nevada, Texas, and Washington—have zero personal income taxes. And all of them have lower per capita tax burdens than California. Why would anyone leave California? One clue may be the Golden State's high tax rates. Perhaps the incomes traveled to where the taxes are lower.

But California is an interesting case. California lost the most AGI between 1995 and 2010 than any state except New York, and three of the top 10 MSAs that lost the most AGI during that period are in California: the Los Angeles MSA, the San Jose MSA, and the San Francisco MSA, which all together lost a staggering $54 billion. However, one of the biggest MSA "winners" in terms of a positive gain of aggregate income is also in California: the Riverside-San Bernardino-Ontario MSA, which gained $11.1 billion. That's interesting, so let's take a closer look.

THE RIVERSIDE MSA

The Riverside MSA is located directly to the east of Los Angeles and the Los Angeles MSA. Often called the Inland Empire, the Riverside MSA is considered part of the greater Los Angeles area, though the Census Bureau categorizes it as a distinct metropolitan statistical area from the Los Angeles–Long Beach–Santa Ana MSA.

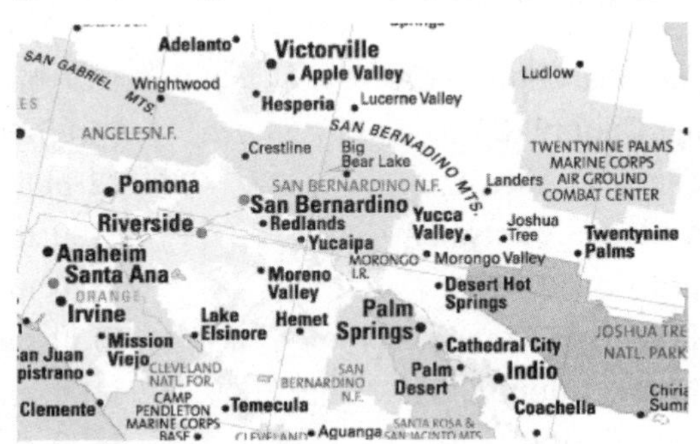

It's a pretty big one, too. The Riverside MSA is the third-most populated area in California and the 13th largest MSA in the U.S., with a population of 4.2 million people. It covers 27,000 square miles, includes the major cities of

Riverside, San Bernardino, and Ontario, and two counties, Riverside and San Bernardino.

The Riverside MSA boasts many attractions, including Joshua Tree National Park, the Coachella Music Festival, and the famed resorts of Palm Springs, Palm Desert, and Rancho Mirage. It has no oceanfront, but it has mountains, deserts, and great proximity to both Los Angeles and the Pacific coast.

Riverside experienced a massive influx of AGI—$11.1 billion—between 1995 and 2010. That's more than twice Riverside County's annual budget of about $4.6 billion.[2]

With that kind of working wealth coming in, the Riverside MSA is obviously a choice destination for a great many people. So where did the money come from? Well, it didn't come very far, that's for sure. Here are the top 10 places that AGI came from:

1. Los Angeles County, CA	$9.7 billion
2. Orange County, CA	$4.1 billion
3. San Diego County, CA	$2 billion
4. Santa Clara County, CA	$190 million
5. Ventura County, CA	$140 million
6. San Francisco County, CA	$130 million
7. San Mateo County, CA	$100 million
8. Alameda County, CA	$100 million
9. Cook County, IL	$70 million
10. Contra Costa County, CA	$70 million

Far and away, the lion's share of the AGI came from Los Angeles County and Orange County, which together comprise the Los Angeles MSA. So, can we gather that people are leaving the Los Angeles MSA but want to stay near LA? Maybe. There are probably a lot of factors, including real estate availability, affordable housing, local taxes, etc.

In terms of real estate, in August 2012, the median price for a home in Los Angeles was $315,000 while the median price for a home in Riverside was $191,800, about 30 percent lower.[3] Taxes may be another reason. Since the federal and state taxes are the same, local taxes may be a factor. Perhaps people can work in LA and enjoy all that the area has to offer but live more affordably in Riverside. Whatever the case, Riverside enjoyed an influx of $11.1 billion in adjusted gross income. Good for them.

Sadly, the rest of the state didn't fare so well. Despite Riverside's incredible gain (which basically came from within the state) California still lost $31.8 billion in AGI from 1995 to 2010. And three other of its MSAs got hammered. Let's start with Riverside's neighbor, the LA MSA.

THE LOS ANGELES MSA

This one's a biggie. The Los Angeles-Long Beach-Santa Ana MSA is the second largest in the country, right behind New York, with 12.8 million people, covering 4,850 square miles. Just two counties comprise the LA MSA, Los Angeles County and Orange County. (Los Angeles County happens to be the most populous county in the United States, with almost 10 million people.)

Major cities in this MSA include Anaheim, Burbank, Huntington Beach, Irvine, Laguna Beach, Long Beach, Los Angeles, Newport Beach, Pasadena, Pomona, Redondo Beach, and San Fernando. This is the California of Beverly Hills, Hollywood, Malibu, and Santa Monica.

As great as it is, it lost about $31.5 billion in AGI between 1995 and 2010—more than four times what all eight *Harry Potter* films grossed combined.[4] That is a lot of money, and here's where it went:

1. Riverside County, CA (Riverside MSA) — $8 billion
2. San Bernardino County, CA (Riverside MSA) — $5.8 billion
3. Clark County, NV (Las Vegas MSA) — $3.2 billion
4. Ventura County, CA (Oxnard MSA) — $2.5 billion
5. San Diego County, CA (San Diego MSA) — $2.3 billion
6. Maricopa County, AZ (Phoenix MSA) — $2 billion
7. Kern County, CA (Bakersfield MSA) — $730 million
8. Santa Barbara County, CA (Santa Barbara MSA) — $650 million
9. San Luis Obispo County, CA (San Luis Obispo MSA) — $620 million
10. King County, WA (Seattle MSA) — $600 million

The bulk of it stayed close by. Of the $26.4 billion represented here, $20.6 billion stayed in California; $13.8 billion of that went to the Riverside MSA alone. Nevada, Arizona, and Washington State each saw a pretty healthy gain of $3.2 billion, $2 billion, and $600 million respectively. Here are the tax facts for those states:

Nevada

- Top state personal income tax rate: 0 percent
- State-local tax burden: 8.2 percent
- Taxes paid per capita: $3,297
- Rank: 42

Arizona

- Top state personal income tax rate: 4.54 percent
- State-local tax burden: 8.4 percent
- Taxes paid per capita: $3,006
- Rank: 40

Washington

- Top state personal income tax rate: 0 percent
- State-local tax burden: 9.3 percent
- Taxes paid per capita: $4,261
- Rank: 28

All a lot lower than California's. Let's look at the next California MSA to lose massive aggregate income, San Jose.

SAN JOSE-SUNNYVALE-SANTA CLARA MSA

When you think of this MSA, think Silicon Valley. Think Cupertino, the headquarters of Apple. Think Los Altos, Los Gatos, Palo Alto, and Stanford University. Located just south of San Francisco, the San Jose MSA is considered part of the San Francisco Bay Area, though it is a distinct metropolitan statistical area, its own MSA.

The San Jose MSA is composed of two counties, San Benito and Santa Clara, and has a population of 1.8 million. Despite being the high-tech hub of the United States, home to venture capitalists, big-thinkers (Stanford!), and the world's most valuable company (Apple), the San Jose MSA lost a whopping $12.3 billion dollars, about a billion dollars more than Apple's 2012 second-quarter profits.[5] That's a lot of iPhones.

Why is San Jose losing so much? And where did it go? Here are the top 10 destinations for that AGI:

1. Alameda County, CA (San Francisco MSA) — $1.2 billion
2. Placer County, CA (Sacramento MSA) — $810 million
3. San Joaquin County, CA (Stockton MSA) — $800 million
4. San Francisco County, CA (San Francisco MSA) — $710 million
5. Sacramento County, CA (Sacramento MSA) — $690 million

6. San Diego County, CA (San Diego MSA) $660 million
7. Contra Costa County, CA (San Francisco MSA) $630 million
8. Maricopa County, AZ (Phoenix MSA) $460 million
9. Santa Cruz County, CA (Santa Cruz MSA) $440 million
10. Clark County, NV (Las Vegas MSA) $430 million

Interesting. Most of it stayed right there in California. However, nearly $900 million went to two high-growth cities, Phoenix and Las Vegas, both of which are emerging as new alternatives for Silicon Valley executives.

Let's look at the last California MSA to lose working wealth, San Francisco.

SAN FRANCISCO-OAKLAND-FREMONT MSA

The San Francisco MSA has a population of about 4.3 million people and includes five counties:

- Alameda County
- Contra Costa County
- Marin County
- San Francisco County
- San Mateo County

It's a very diverse area culturally and geographically, and includes the cities of Berkeley, Half Moon Bay, Menlo

Park, Oakland, San Francisco, San Ramon, and Walnut Creek, to name a few. It's the Bay Area in all its glory.

It also lost $10.2 billion between 1995 and 2010 in AGI. Here's where it went:

1. San Joaquin County, CA (Stockton MSA) $1.6 billion
2. Sonoma County, CA (Santa Rosa MSA) $1.4 billion
3. Sacramento County, CA (Sacramento MSA) $1.2 billion
4. Solano County, CA (Vallejo MSA) $1.1 billion
5. Placer County, CA (Sacramento MSA) $1 billion
6. Maricopa County, AZ (Phoenix MSA) $760 million
7. Clark County, NV (Las Vegas MSA) $660 million
8. Washoe County, NV (Reno MSA) $600 million
9. San Diego County, CA (San Diego MSA) $570 million
10. El Dorado County, CA (Sacramento MSA) $490 million

Again, the bulk of the AGI stayed right there in California, just not in the Bay Area.

Even though the California MSAs saw a lot of movement between them, the state of California still saw a net loss of–and this is a real loss, not a movement between its MSAs–$31.8 billion in AGI from 1995 to 2010.

California's GDP is the ninth largest in the world; it's bigger than Russia's and almost as big as Italy's.[6] California is a powerhouse, to be sure, but no state can survive for long that loses more than $2 billion a year in working wealth. Its rankings are pretty bleak, too. The 2012 ALEC-Laffer State Economic Competitiveness Index ranked California 47th out of the 50 states in economic performance and 38th in the country in economic outlook. Not exactly an optimistic outlook. Most of California's AGI moved to Arizona and Nevada, so let's look at those states next.

Scan here for supplemental and additional material, illustrations, video, and other information.

Chapter Seven Endnotes:

[1] DreamWorks Animation SKG market value as of October 2012, Forbes.com.

[2] Riverside County's FY2013 budget, http://www.countyofriverside.us/export/sites/default/government/budget/FY2012_2103_recommended/FY13RecommendedBudgetFinal.pdf.

[3] Los Angeles median home price figure, http://www.latimes.com/business/money/la-fi-mo-home-sales-20121012,0,931356.story; Riverside figure, http://www.zillow.com/local-info/CA-Riverside-home-value/r_47401/.

[4] *Harry Potter* films total gross, http://www.the-numbers.com/movies/series/HarryPotter.php.

[5] Apple 2012 second quarter profits: http://www.apple.com/pr/library/2012/04/24Apple-Reports-Second-Quarter-Results.html.

[6] GDPs, http://www.ccsce.com/PDF/Numbers-Sept-2012-CA-Economy-Rankings-2011.pdf.

Chapter Eight

A Personal Perspective

A LONELY WALK IN THE DESERT TURNS CROWDED

By Niger Innis

Historian John Steele Gordon elegantly wrote, "There is probably no 150,000 square miles on the planet more God-favored than California. Its geographic diversity, its climate, its scenic wonders, its incredible mineral wealth, its agricultural abundance are all without equal. No wonder it was a magnet for immigrants for 150 years."[1]

For the longest time, some of the greatest arguments in favor of California neighbors Nevada and Arizona were their proximity to the Golden State. With the latter filled with the nation's most ambitious, talented,

and innovative people, Nevada and Arizona couldn't help but thrive simply for being next door. Also, flush with the monetary fruits of all their economic creativity, Californians would travel to Nevada for skiing and to Arizona for golf.

So influential and important was California that even when it failed, its corrections of its failures had national–perhaps global–implications. Thanks to ever-increasing property taxes in the 1970s, California's reputation for growth fell a notch as the greedy hand of its government reached deeper and deeper into the pockets of its citizenry. The result was Proposition 13, a referendum that held the line on taxes, and which is said to have sparked both a national and global revolt against rapacious politicians.

Specifically, California has always been a leader and a trendsetter, though now it is setting trends that it would rather not claim. California has sparked a national trend whereby "money walks" to more tax-friendly locales; in California's case many of its best and brightest have ventured into an increasingly crowded desert for the more pro-business climes of Nevada and Arizona.

California doesn't have a monopoly on great weather, and with Arizona's state personal income tax rate topping out at 4.5 percent (versus 13.3 percent for California), its similarly sunny skies, eminently more affordable housing, and audibly more pro-business stance have proven increasingly attractive to Golden Staters who've grown tired of being fleeced. As for Nevada, its lack of a state income tax says it all.

The Founding Fathers properly viewed the states as autonomous entities wherein the vast majority of legislation—tax and otherwise—would occur. Supreme Court Justice Louis Brandeis believed that states were to serve as "laboratories" of ideas. At present, it seems the experiment between low- and high-tax states has produced for the political class a very clear conclusion: taxes matter, and states whose legislatures strive to keep them low will be the recipients of ambitious human capital eager to escape the long arms of revenue-hungry politicians.

The irony of California's human capital outflow is that its own brilliant citizens arguably created the economic conditions that made it possible. Indeed, thanks to technological innovations of the computer and Internet variety, largely hatched

in Silicon Valley, location is increasingly irrelevant. Thanks to California-based companies like oDesk, the computer programmer in Sedona can work side by side with the engineer in Shanghai.

Though still very much a place full of great minds, Silicon Valley is presently innovating itself into a symbol such that top technological minds will no longer need to live there in order to work there. Death of distance? Yes, and California erased distance as a major economic factor. Arizona and Nevada are the certain beneficiaries of the genius of California technologists.

What's not advanced in this most advanced of states are its policies of taxation. While the technology that emanates from California continues to astound and change the world, the state's legislature regresses and foists on the world's most talented an increasingly confiscatory tax code that tells them "innovate all you like, but a big bill awaits from Sacramento when you're done." Sacramento's egregious errors on the tax front redound to Arizona and Nevada, sending their way the most precious capital of all: human capital.

The desert is growing very crowded indeed.

In the final analysis, America faces a critical fork in the road, one that will inevitably determine the economic fate of our nation. Which "West" will America choose? Which will prevail? Will it be the West of California, where we become just another Western European-style social democracy, following the trend of an ever-increasing government, an entitlement-dependent citizenry, and the confiscatory tax policies that follow? Or will it be the economic liberties of the "other" West–Nevada, Arizona, and Texas–states that have all planted the seeds for dynamic economic growth?

We are at the crossroads, and this is the choice.

~

Niger Innis is the national spokesman for the Congress of Racial Equality.

Chapter Eight Personal Perspective Endnote:

[1] John Steele Gordon, "The Rise and Needless Decline of the Golden State," the *Wall Street Journal* (July 5, 2011), http://online.wsj.com/article/SB10001424052702304314404576413873080595908.html.

Chapter Eight

THE DESERT STATES THRIVE

Arizona's and Nevada's Extraordinary Growth

Despite being the center of much of the country's commerce and culture–Silicon Valley, Hollywood–California saw a massive amount of aggregate income leave its borders between 1995 and 2010. Working wealth fled the Golden State. But the rest of the West didn't fare as badly. In fact, many western states positively thrived, as California's loss was their gain.

Let's look at two states and their MSAs that saw enormous net influxes of AGI, much of it from California: Arizona and the Phoenix MSA and Nevada and the Las Vegas MSA.

ARIZONA AND THE PHOENIX MSA

Arizona is the sixth largest state in the U.S. in terms of size and the 16th in terms of population, with about 6.5 million people. It was the last contiguous state to be added to the union, in 1912. The state is home to Flagstaff, Scottsdale, Tucson, and its largest city and capital, Phoenix.

As anyone who has been there knows, Arizona is a predominantly dry, desert state, punctuated by beautiful, jagged mountain ranges, gorgeous national parks, and stunning natural landmarks, like the Superstition Mountains, the Red Rocks of Sedona, Meteor Crater, Joshua Tree, the Petrified Forest, and, of course, the Grand Canyon.

Arizona is considered by many to have a very favorable climate (at least in the winter). The air is dry and the average temperature is 72.8 degrees, making the state well liked by locals, retirees, and vacationers alike.

Apparently, Arizona's climate is also a welcome one for working wealth. According to the IRS, between 1995 and 2010, Arizona saw a net gain of $24.5 billion in AGI from other states. That's a massive influx of aggregate income, equal to about three times the entire state's FY2013 budget of $8 billion.[1]

Why did Arizona see such a massive influx of wealth? Aside from the weather and stunning desert vistas, what makes Arizona so attractive? Well, in addition to its natural charms, the state also offers a very favorable tax climate. Arizona has one of the lowest per capita tax burdens in the country and a relatively low state personal income tax rate. Here are Arizona's tax facts:

ARIZONA TAX FACTS	
	Top personal income tax rate: 4.54%
	State-local tax burden: 8.4% Taxes paid per capita: $3,006 Rank: 40
	Net gain of AGI: $24.5 billion

Maybe that's why so much money moved to the Grand Canyon State—dry desert air and low taxes. Sounds like a great combination. Where did the money come from? Here are the top five states from which Arizona gained the most AGI:

- California, $6.3 billion
- Illinois, $2.4 billion
- New York, $1.4 billion
- Michigan, $1.2 billion
- Minnesota, $1 billion

And let's look at the tax situations in those five states:

California

- Top personal income tax rate: 13.3 percent
- State-local tax burden: 11.2 percent
- Taxes paid per capita: $4,934
- Rank: 4

Illinois

- Top personal income tax rate: 5 percent
- State-local tax burden: 10.2 percent
- Taxes paid per capita: $4,512
- Rank: 11

New York

- Top personal income tax rate: 8.82 percent
- State-local tax burden: 12.8 percent
- Taxes paid per capita: $6,375
- Rank: 1 (highest in the nation)

Michigan

- Top personal income tax rate: 4.35 percent
- State-local tax burden: 9.8 percent
- Taxes paid per capita: $3,503
- Rank: 18

Minnesota

- Top personal income tax rate: 7.85 percent
- State-local tax burden: 10.8 percent
- Taxes pad per capita: $4,727
- Rank: 7

Every state that lost AGI to Arizona has higher state-local tax burdens, and all but one higher income taxes. No wonder so much working wealth moved to Arizona. It likes it there.

Let's look at the state that sent the most aggregate income to Arizona: California. California, you'll recall from the last chapter, lost a total of $31.8 billion in AGI between 1995 and 2010. Twenty percent of it went to Arizona. California was Arizona's single greatest source of AGI over that period. According to IRS statistics, 322,454 people moved to Arizona from California between 1995 and 2010, bringing with them over $14 billion in AGI.

Of the top 10 counties in the United States that sent AGI to Arizona between 1995 and 2010, six are in California. Here they are:

Los Angeles County (LA MSA):

- Number of people who migrated to Arizona: 75,762
- AGI loss: $3.2 billion

San Diego County (San Diego MSA):

- Number of people who migrated to Arizona: 46,889
- AGI loss: $1.9 billion

Orange County (LA MSA):

- Number of people who migrated to Arizona: 34,604
- AGI loss: $1.8 billion

Santa Clara County (San Jose MSA):

- Number of people who migrated to Arizona: 14,511
- AGI loss: $1.1 billion

Riverside County (Riverside MSA):

- Number of people who migrated to Arizona: 24,318
- AGI loss: $965 million

San Bernardino County (Riverside MSA):

- Number of people who migrated to Arizona: 25,114
- AGI loss: $875 million

Amazing. If I were California, I'd be dreaming of a way to get that money back.

Now that we know how much money moved into the state of Arizona and where it came from, let's look at where it landed. The predominant recipient was the Phoenix MSA, which enjoyed the biggest net gain in AGI of any MSA in the country from 1995 to 2010—$17.1 billion.

PHOENIX RISES

I'll say it again: the Phoenix MSA—officially Phoenix-Mesa-Glendale—gained $17.1 billion in AGI between 1995 and 2010. That's 10 times the market value of the Arizona Cardinals, the Arizona Diamondbacks, and the Phoenix Suns combined,[2] and enough to fund the entire $8 billion state budget of Arizona for two years, with plenty left over.

So, why Phoenix? Well, why not? As we know, the climate is hospitable. The air is dry, the weather is great, the area is culturally rich and diverse, and the geography is varied and beautiful, with forests to the north and the high desert to the south. And we know the taxes are relatively low.

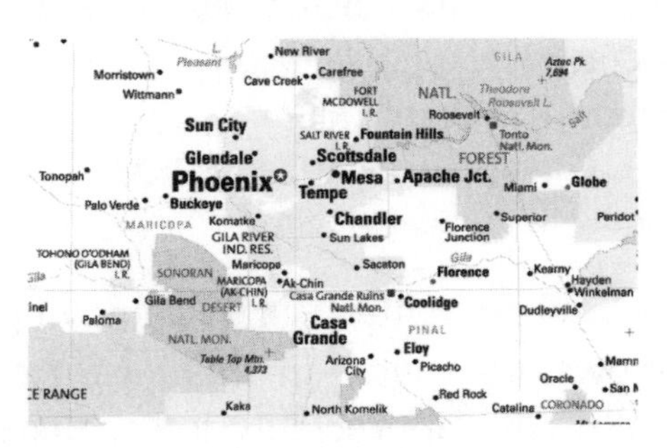

The Phoenix MSA is composed of two counties, Maricopa and Pinal, and covers a very large area, about 16,600 square miles. The MSA includes the cities of Chandler, Glendale, Mesa, Paradise Valley, Phoenix, Scottsdale, Sun City, and Tempe, among others.

The Phoenix MSA has a population of 4.2 million, the 14th largest in the country. Two-thirds of the residents of the state of Arizona live in the Phoenix MSA, which, according to the Census Bureau, grew by a staggering 45 percent between 1990 and 2010, from 2.2 million to 4.2 million people. Phoenix is booming.

In addition to an incredible influx of people, the Phoenix MSA also enjoyed a massive influx of $17.1 billion in AGI between 1995 and 2010. As we know, about 20 percent of that AGI came from California. Here is exactly where the income that came to the Phoenix MSA originated, by county:

1. Los Angeles County, CA (LA MSA) $1.5 billion
2. Cook County, IL (Chicago MSA) $1 billion
3. Orange County, CA (LA MSA) $660 million
4. Pima County, AZ (Tucson MSA) $490 million
5. Santa Clara County, CA (San Jose MSA) $470 million
6. Hennepin County, MN (Minneapolis MSA) $370 million
7. DuPage County, IL (Chicago MSA) $340 million
8. King County, WA (Seattle MSA) $310 million
9. San Diego County, CA (San Diego MSA) $310 million
10. Lake County, IL (Chicago MSA) $290 million

Again, we see a clear pattern of AGI moving from high-tax states to lower-tax ones—in this case Arizona, which welcomes wealth with appreciably lower taxes. If we look at the biggest source of the Phoenix MSA's gain, we again see California, and, again, these four California counties in the top 10:

- Los Angeles County (LA MSA)
- Orange County (LA MSA)
- Santa Clara County (San Jose MSA)
- San Diego County (San Diego MSA)

California's loss was Arizona's gain. Let's look at another western state (which happens to be another California neighbor) that also enjoyed billions in the movement of aggregate income, Nevada.

NEVADA HITS THE JACKPOT

Nevada is a large state by area, ranking seventh in the nation in size, with about 100,000 square miles. It's one of the least populated, though, with just 2.7 million people.

And just like Arizona, Nevada enjoyed an immense influx of both people (275,000) and AGI ($15.9 billion) between 1995 and 2010. That's just about twice the 2011 gross revenue of MGM Resorts International, which owns the Bellagio, Circus Circus, Mandalay Bay, MGM Grand, and a host of other resorts and casinos around the world.[3] That's some jackpot.

But, like Arizona, Nevada offers a welcoming climate. It's the driest state in the U.S., averaging only about seven inches of rain a year and an average temperature of 67.5 degrees. And the taxes are some of the lowest in the country:

NEVADA TAX FACTS	
	Top personal income tax rate: 0%
	State-local tax burden: 8.2% Taxes paid per capita: $3,297 Rank: 42
	Net gain of AGI: $15.9 billion

Where did the $15.9 billion come from? Here:

- California, $8.2 billion
- Illinois, $913 million
- New York, $896 million
- Michigan, $531 million
- Ohio, $464 million

And, again, we see the same four states that sent AGI to Arizona (California, Illinois, New York, and Michigan) along with a new one, Ohio. Here are Ohio's tax facts:

OHIO TAX FACTS	
	Top personal income tax rate: 5.93%
	State-local tax burden: 9.7% Taxes paid per capita: $3,563 Rank: 20
	Net loss of AGI: $17.1 billion

Nevada has no state personal income tax rate and a lower per capita state tax burden than any of those. Like Arizona, perhaps the low taxes contributed to the attraction of moving there. Let's look at where the income came from:

1.	Los Angeles County, CA (LA MSA)	$2.8 billion
2.	Orange County, CA (LA MSA)	$1.1 billion
3.	Santa Clara County, CA (San Jose MSA)	$960 million
4.	San Diego County, CA (San Diego MSA)	$586 million
5.	Cook County, IL (Chicago MSA)	$571 million
6.	San Bernardino County, CA (Riverside MSA)	$502 million
7.	Alameda County, CA (San Francisco MSA)	$481 million
8.	Contra Costa County, CA (San Francisco MSA)	$427 million
9.	San Mateo County, CA (San Francisco MSA)	$338 million
10.	Honolulu County, HI (Honolulu MSA)	$323 million

Again, the bulk of the movement to Nevada, in terms of both people and AGI, is coming from right next door:

California. Working wealth moved from one of the highest tax states in the country to one of the lowest.

Let's look at the Las Vegas MSA, which enjoyed the third highest net gain of any MSA in the country—$11.6 billion in AGI.

VIVA LAS VEGAS

The largest city in Nevada is Las Vegas. The Las Vegas-Paradise MSA includes Clark County, has 1.9 million people, and covers 7,891 square miles.

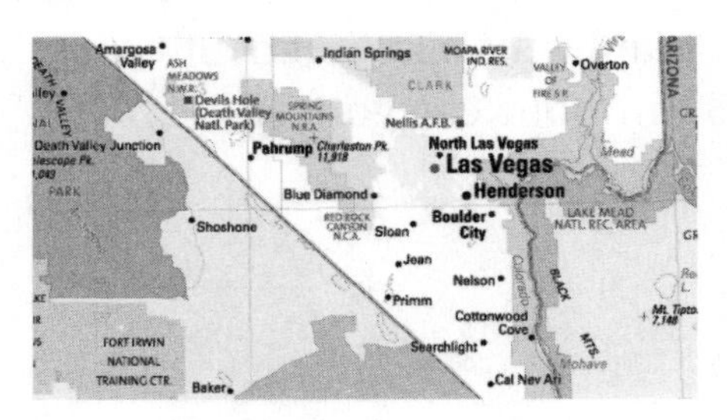

Las Vegas gained $11.6 billion in AGI from 1995 to 2010. That's about four and a half times the net worth of one of Las Vegas' richest men, Steve Wynn, chairman and CEO of Wynn Resorts.[4]

But Vegas didn't win that money at the tables. That money moved to the Las Vegas MSA from other places. Which other places? Here's exactly where it came from:

1.	Los Angeles County, CA (LA MSA)	$2.3 billion
2.	Orange County, CA (LA MSA)	$860 million
3.	Cook County, IL (Chicago MSA)	$540 million

4.	San Diego County, CA (San Diego MSA)	$460 million
5.	Santa Clara County, CA (San Jose MSA)	$420 million
6.	San Bernardino County, CA (Riverside MSA)	$410 million
7.	Honolulu County, HI (Honolulu MSA)	$320 million
8.	Alameda County, CA (San Francisco MSA)	$220 million
9.	Ventura County, CA (Ventura MSA)	$220 million
10.	Johnson County, KS (Kansas City MSA)	$180 million

I sound like a broken record, but, again, we see California–Nevada's neighbor–losing the most AGI. If Nevada "won" that working wealth, it did so by offering a far more favorable tax climate. Arizona, too. In fact, Arizona ranked 11th out of 50 states in economic performance and ninth out of 50 in economic outlook on the 2012 ALEC-Laffer State Economic Competitiveness Index. Nevada ranked 18th in both categories.

It's no wonder that Zappos CEO Tony Hsieh is making an investment of $350 million to move his company headquarters from suburban Henderson, Nevada, to downtown Las Vegas. He wants to move his HQ to a vibrant MSA, and he is putting his money where his mouth is.

Let's turn now to another part of the country, which, unfortunately, hasn't done as well as these desert states–the Midwest.

Scan here for supplemental and additional material, illustrations, video, and other information.

Chapter Eight Endnotes:

[1] Arizona state budget, Sunshinereview.org.

[2] Team values, Forbes.com, "The Business of Football," http://www.forbes.com/nfl-valuations/list/; "The Business of Baseball," http://www.forbes.com/mlb-valuations/list/; and "The Business of Basketball," http://www.forbes.com/nba-valuations/list/.

[3] MGM Resorts International 2011 gross revenue, http://finapps.forbes.com/finapps/jsp/finance/compinfo/IncomeStatement.jsp?tkr=mgm&period=qtr.

[4] Steve Wynn's net worth as of September 2012, http://www.forbes.com/profile/steve-wynn/.

Chapter Nine

A Personal Perspective

BIG SHOULDERS AREN'T ENOUGH ANYMORE

By Rex Sinquefield

"Chicago"

Hog Butcher for the World,
Tool Maker, Stacker of Wheat,
Player with Railroads and the Nation's Freight Handler;
Stormy, husky, brawling,
City of the Big Shoulders.

–Carl Sandburg

As Carl Sandburg points out in his famed 1916 poem, there is much to appreciate about the city of Chicago. My personal connection to the city goes back to when my wife Jeanne and I attended graduate school at the University of Chicago. It

was a time when the free-market and investment theorists of the day were creating fertile ground for the development of bright, young minds studying business and economics. Each morning, I stepped out of our Hyde Park house to fetch the daily newspaper and greet our neighbors, several of whom would go on to become Nobel Prize winners in economics.

Indeed, Chicago's industrial and cultural history is rich, evidenced by the veritable showcase of late nineteenth- and twentieth-century industrial architecture that frames Michigan Avenue and the Chicago River. Today, its cultural and entertainment offerings are vibrant, teeming with world-class art, theater, and music institutions and a cutting-edge food scene. This City of Big Shoulders appears to be capable of successfully managing any brutal turn of events that it may face, as it did the Great Chicago Fire and the Chicago Flood.

Not so in the twenty-first century.

I can draw from my own personal experience to provide a perfect example of how Illinois tax policy has failed one of the state's greatest assets, delivering the kind of economic blows that would

render Sugar Ray Robinson, Rocky Marciano, and Floyd Patterson weak-kneed and staggering.

Expanding Dimensional Fund Advisor's (DFA) Chicago office was on our A-list, as my co-founder in the company, David Booth, and I grew DFA offices in other markets. In the last few years, we have grown DFA from $100 billion in managed assets to more than $260 billion, and we now have offices in Santa Monica, Sydney, London, and Vancouver. We also considered moving to Kansas City, Missouri, as David was raised in Lawrence, Kansas, and wanted to set up shop closer to his hometown.

So instead of choosing one of two areas of the country—Illinois or Kansas—with which DFA leadership has strong personal ties and would have preferred, why did DFA relocate 25 employees to Austin, Texas?

Austin's success in recruiting DFA was the result of its effort to develop its financial services industry. DFA's decision to move there was due in large part to that effort and to Texas' pro-business environment, which includes zero state income tax. Moving from California to Texas and avoiding higher tax destinations, such as Missouri and Illinois, gave our

employees an immediate raise in salary. Soon afterward, we more than doubled the size of that office.

As Travis H. Brown clearly points out in this chapter of *How Money Walks*, it is reasonable to argue that Chicago's blues can be felt across the Midwest. It can easily be traced to other midwestern states that are pummeling residents and employers with painful and fateful tax policies. In the last 15 years or so, about $80 billion in AGI moved out of 12 midwestern states, much of it headed for lower tax states in other parts of the country. Illinois lost the most—a staggering *$26 billion.*

What is clear is the fact that many of those things that attract workers and companies to relocate to an area cannot beat the harmful effects of bad tax policies and cannot compete with states that offer friendlier tax policies.

In "Chicago" Carl Sandburg challenges us, "Come and show me another city with lifted head singing so proud to be alive and coarse and strong and cunning." One need only point to how Chicago's state government is doing by its key economic driver, landing 48th in state economic per-

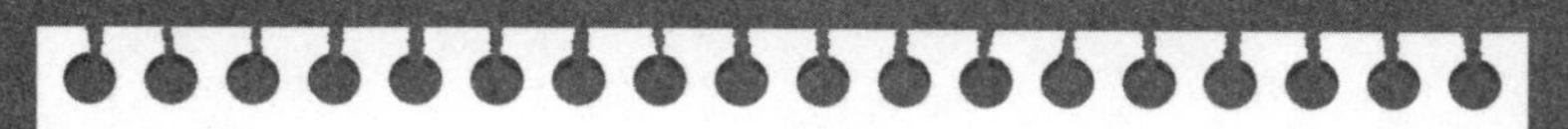

formance and 48th in state economic outlook, according to *Rich States, Poor States*. Then, watch how people, and their money, move across our country to communities such as Austin, Las Vegas, and Tampa, whose state pride and cunning policies are making economic champions out of their urban areas.

~

Rex Sinquefield is the co-founder of Dimensional Fund Advisors and the co-founder and president of the Show-Me Institute, a free-market think tank based in St. Louis. He and his wife, Dr. Jeanne Sinquefield, are the founders of the Chess Club and Scholastic Center and the World Chess Hall of Fame in St. Louis, and are major supporters of education and the arts. He is a life trustee of DePaul University and received the 2012 John D. Levy Human Relations Award from the American Jewish Committee. He is a regular contributor to Forbes.com.

Chapter Nine

MIDWEST BLUES

Humble times for a once great region

It's amazing when you start to see migratory patterns emerge. From the preceding chapters, there appears to be a strong correlation between taxes and the movement of aggregate income. Basically, working wealth appears to be leaving high-tax states in favor of lower-tax ones, especially those with low or no personal income taxes. That was certainly the case in California, Connecticut, Illinois, Kansas, Maryland, Massachusetts, Michigan, New Jersey, New York, Ohio, Pennsylvania, and Washington, DC, all of which lost billions in AGI to states like Arizona, Florida, and Nevada.

We are going to turn now to the Midwest, which, sadly, is a bit like California and the East Coast in that it has lost billions in AGI to other states.

The Midwest is defined by the Census Bureau as these 12 states: Illinois, Indiana, Iowa, Kansas, Michigan, Minnesota, Missouri, Nebraska, North Dakota, Ohio, South Dakota, and Wisconsin.

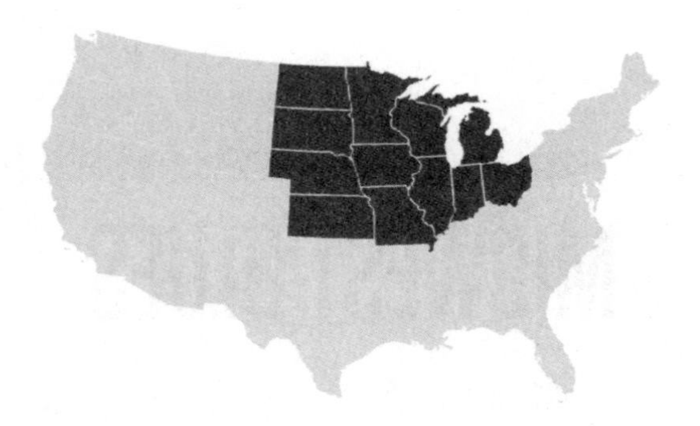

Here's how those states fared between 1995 and 2010 in terms of income migration, along with their tax facts.

ILLINOIS TAX FACTS	
	Top personal income tax rate: 5%
	State-local tax burden: 10.2 percent Taxes paid per capita: $4,512 Rank: 11
	Net loss of AGI: $26.1 billion

INDIANA TAX FACTS	
	Top personal income tax rate: 3.4%
	State-local tax burden: 9.6% Taxes paid per capita: $3,294 Rank: 23
	Net loss of AGI: $3.9 billion

IOWA TAX FACTS	
	Top personal income tax rate: 8.98%
	State-local tax burden: 9.6% Taxes paid per capita: $3,660 Rank: 23
	Net loss of AGI: $3.2 billion

KANSAS TAX FACTS	
	Top personal income tax rate: 4.9%
	State-local tax burden: 9.7% Taxes paid per capita: $3,802 Rank: 22
	Net loss of AGI: $3 billion

MICHIGAN TAX FACTS	
	Top personal income tax rate: 4.35%
	State-local tax burden: 9.8% Taxes paid per capita: $3,503 Rank: 18
	Net loss of AGI: $15.6 billion

MINNESOTA TAX FACTS	
	Top personal income tax rate: 7.85%
	State-local tax burden: 10.8% Taxes paid per capita: $4,727 Rank: 7
	Net loss of AGI: $4.1 billion

MISSOURI TAX FACTS	
	Top personal income tax rate: 6%
	State-local tax burden: 9% Taxes paid per capita: $3,328 Rank: 34
	Net loss of AGI: $1.6 billion

NEBRASKA TAX FACTS	
	Top personal income tax rate: 6.84%
	State-local tax burden: 9.7% Taxes paid per capita: $3,853 Rank: 21
	Net loss of AGI: $2.3 billion

NORTH DAKOTA TAX FACTS	
	Top personal income tax rate: 3.99%
	State-local tax burden: 8.9% Taxes paid per capita: $3,733 Rank: 35
	Net loss of AGI: $1.2 billion

OHIO TAX FACTS	
	Top personal income tax rate: 5.93%
	State-local tax burden: 9.7% Taxes paid per capita: $3,563 Rank: 20
	Net loss of AGI: $17.1 billion

SOUTH DAKOTA TAX FACTS	
	Top personal income tax rate: 0%
	State-local tax burden: 7.6% Taxes paid per capita: $3,035 Rank: 49
	Net gain of AGI: $528 million

WISCONSIN TAX FACTS
Top personal income tax rate: 7.75%
State-local tax burden: 11.1% Taxes paid per capita: $4,379 Rank: 5
Net loss of AGI: $2.5 billion

All together, between 1995 and 2010, about $80.1 billion in AGI moved out of (and between, in a few cases) these 12 midwestern states. That's about the market value of two of the Midwest's oldest companies, John Deere and Caterpillar, combined.[1] Eighty billion dollars would buy a lot of tractors.

IMAGE CREDIT: SHUTTERSTOCK.COM

Illinois lost the most—a staggering $26 billion. And where did the Midwest's AGI go? Well, some of that $80.1 billion stayed in the Midwest, but on balance, most of it went to other states. And, as we can see from the IRS data, three states received the lion's share—$35 billion—of the AGI:

- Florida, $21.1 billion
- Arizona, $7.3 billion
- Texas, $6.6 billion

Once again, good for Florida, Arizona, and Texas, each of which has lower taxes than any state in the Midwest, with one exception–South Dakota.

South Dakota is the only midwestern state to see a net gain in AGI. Granted, South Dakota's gain was in millions not billions of dollars, but as a very small state with a population of just 824,000, a gain of $528 million is tremendous. That's about $35 million a year, or two times the state's annual budget for agriculture and natural resources.[2]

And why would South Dakota see a gain when the other 11 midwestern states suffered losses in the billions of dollars? Well, everyone loves the Badlands and the Black Hills, Deadwood, Mt. Rushmore, and Wall Drug, but it probably has more to do with the tax situation: South Dakota has zero personal income taxes and the second lowest per capita tax burden in the country, even lower than Arizona, Florida, and Texas. Clearly, people who move to South Dakota aren't just coming for the Corn Palace.

In fact, South Dakota ranks very high on the 2012 ALEC-Laffer State Economic Competitiveness Index, which ranked the state second in the country in economic performance and seventh in economic outlook. Things look very good for South Dakota. Here are the ALEC-Laffer rankings for the other 11 midwestern states:

STATE	ECONOMIC PERFORMANCE	ECONOMIC OUTLOOK
Illinois	48	48
Indiana	46	24
Iowa	28	22
Kansas	39	26
Michigan	50	17
Minnesota	41	41
Missouri	38	7
Nebraska	20	31
North Dakota	4	5
Ohio	49	37
South Dakota	7	2
Wisconsin	42	32

With the exception of North and South Dakota, the overall economic performance of the Midwest is pretty bleak. However, in terms of economic outlook, things look pretty good for North Dakota, South Dakota, and Missouri. It's not surprising that the states with the worst economic performance and outlook are also the ones that also lost the most working wealth: Illinois lost $26.1 billion, Ohio lost $17.1 billion, and Michigan lost $15.6 billion.

Three of the top 10 MSAs that lost the most AGI from 1995 to 2010 happen to be in those three states: Chicago, Detroit, and Cleveland. Let's begin in the Windy City.

THE WINDY CITY BLOWS IT

Chicago is one of the greatest cities in the world. Dubbed

the Second City, denizens of the Windy City know their town to be extraordinary in every way. Perched on the shores of Lake Michigan, Chicago has everything going for it: world-class architecture, famed universities, great sports teams, incredible shopping and dining, and a vibrant city culture second to none.

Chicago, the city proper, has 2.7 million residents, according to the Census Bureau. But the Chicago MSA—officially known as Chicago-Joliet-Naperville, IL-IN-WI—has 9.5 million people and is the third largest metropolitan area in the United States, behind the New York and Los Angeles MSAs. It's a big one, too, covering 7,200 square miles and 14 counties in three states, Illinois, Indiana, and Wisconsin:

- Cook County, IL
- DeKalb County, IL
- DuPage County, IL
- Grundy County, IL
- Jasper County, IN
- Kane County, IL
- Kendall County, IL
- Kenosha County, WI
- Lake County, IL
- Lake County, IN
- McHenry County, IL

- Newton County, IN
- Porter County, IN
- Will County, IL

The Chicago MSA lost a staggering $21.1 billion in AGI between 1995 and 2010. That's about 7.8 times the $2.7 billion net worth of Chicago resident, Oprah Winfrey.[3]

Here are the top 10 places where Chicago's AGI moved:

1.	Maricopa County, AZ (Phoenix MSA)	$1.9 billion
2.	Clark County, NV (Las Vegas MSA)	$900 million
3.	Palm Beach County, FL (Miami MSA)	$890 million
4.	Collier County, FL (Naples MSA)	$820 million
5.	Lee County, FL (Cape Coral MSA)	$720 million
6.	Pinellas County, FL (Tampa MSA)	$430 million
7.	Boone County, IL (Rockford MSA)	$400 million
8.	San Diego County, CA (San Diego MSA)	$390 million
9.	New York County, NY (NY MSA)	$390 million
10.	Sarasota County, FL (Sarasota MSA)	$370 million

As we can see, the bulk went south, to Florida, and west, to Arizona and Nevada—all climates that are not just milder in the winter but more hospitable to income, with far lower taxes than Illinois, which has the 11th highest per capita taxes in the country.

We can drill down to each and every one of the 14 counties that make up the Chicago MSA, but let's just look at the biggest one, Cook County. Between 1995 and 2010, Cook County alone lost $1.7 billion in AGI. That's the combined market value of Chicago's beloved NFL team, the Bears, and its famed NBA team, the Bulls.[4]

Chicago is a great metropolitan area, one of the greatest in the world. But clearly, the people who moved out of it between 1995 and 2010, taking over $21 billion in AGI with them, had a change of heart. Could it be the harsh winters and the winds whipping in off the lake? Could it be the rough and tumble political atmosphere for which Chicago is famed? Or could it be the high state taxes—a 5 percent top personal income tax rate contributing to a 10.2 percent state-local tax burden, making it the 11th highest in the country?

It's hard to say, but the data shows a clear movement of working wealth to states with lower tax rates. Opportunity is knocking elsewhere for Bears fans.

Let's turn now to one of Chicago's neighbors, another famed midwestern city, Detroit.

THE MOTOR CITY STALLS

Detroit, Michigan, is as storied as any American city. Long synonymous with the auto industry, Detroit is where it all began: Chrysler, Ford, and General Motors, the Big Three. It's also the birthplace of Barry Gordy and Motown, a record label and musical style that would define more than a generation of music.

Nestled on the banks of Lake Erie, a small harbor's distance from Windsor, Canada, Detroit was once a mighty center of commerce and industry. But the past few decades have been unkind to Detroit, and the area is one of the hardest hit by the recent recession as well as by the overall decline of the American auto industry.

The state of Michigan lost $15.6 billion in AGI between 1995 and 2010. That's about $2 billion more than Kellogg's total 2011 revenue of $13 billion.[5] That's a lot of Froot Loops.

Here are the top 10 states where Michigan's AGI went:

1.	Florida	$4.8 billion
2.	California	$1.3 billion
3.	Texas	$1.2 billion
4.	Arizona	$1.2 billion
5.	North Carolina	$1 billion
6.	Tennessee	$846 million
7.	Georgia	$779 million
8.	South Carolina	$611 million
9.	Illinois	$536 million
10.	Nevada	$531 million

And here are the top 10 counties where that income went:

1.	Maricopa County, AZ (Phoenix MSA)	$942 million
2.	Lee County, FL (Cape Coral MSA)	$617 million
3.	Collier County, FL (Naples MSA)	$565 million
4.	Clark County, NV (Las Vegas MSA)	$466 million
5.	Sarasota County, FL Sarasota MSA)	$381 million
6.	Palm Beach County, FL (Miami MSA)	$337 million
7.	Cook County, IL (Chicago MSA)	$299 million
8.	Pinellas County, FL (Tampa MSA)	$266 million
9.	San Diego County, CA (San Diego MSA)	$237 million
10.	Mecklenburg County, NC (Charlotte MSA)	$219 million

Though a lot of it stayed in the Midwest (and would later leave), much of the AGI went to warmer, more welcoming climates tax-wise—most notably Arizona, Florida, and, again, Nevada.

Now let's look at the Detroit MSA.

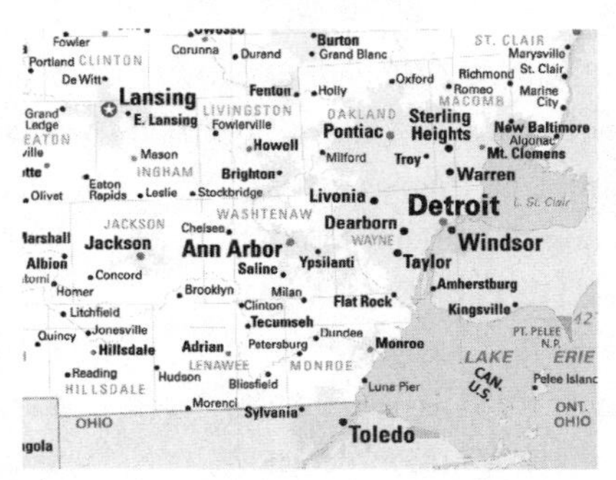

The Detroit-Warren-Livonia MSA is the 12th largest in the country, with a population of about 4.3 million people. According to the Census Bureau, the population of the Detroit MSA has remained relatively flat over the past 20 years: it grew from 4.249 million people in 1990 to 4.453 million people in 2000, before falling back to 4.296 million, a net increase of just 47,000 people in 20 years.

The Detroit MSA covers 3,900 square miles over these six counties:

- Lapeer County
- Livingston County
- Macomb County
- Oakland County
- St. Clair County
- Wayne County

And between 1995 and 2010, it lost $12.5 billion in AGI. That's more than six times the market value of all of Detroit's professional sports teams—the Lions, Tigers, Red Wings, and Pistons—combined.[6]

Here are the top 10 places where that income went:

1.	Maricopa County, AZ (Phoenix MSA)	$560 million
2.	Washtenaw County, MI (Ann Arbor MSA)	$420 million
3.	Collier County, FL (Naples MSA)	$370 million
4.	Genesee County, MI (Flint MSA)	$360 million
5.	Lee County, FL (Cape Coral MSA)	$350 million
6.	Cook County, IL (Chicago MSA)	$320 million
7.	Clark County, NV (Las Vegas MSA)	$320 million
8.	Monroe County, MI (Monroe MSA)	$300 million
9.	Palm Beach County, FL (Miami MSA)	$260 billion
10.	Sarasota County, FL (North Port MSA)	$260 billion

While much of Detroit's income stayed in the state (it moved to neighboring counties) the bulk of it went to Arizona, Florida, and Nevada, states with, as we know, much lower taxes.

Let's stay on Lake Erie and look at another midwestern MSA, Cleveland.

CLEVELAND ISN'T ROCKING

Like Illinois and Michigan, Ohio lost a substantial amount of AGI between 1995 and 2010—$17.1 billion, about eight times the $2.1 billion endowment of Ohio State University.[7] Here are the top five places it went:

1.	Florida	$5.9 billion
2.	North Carolina	$1.4 billion
3.	Texas	$1.1 billion
4.	South Carolina	$1.1 billion
5.	Arizona	$996 million

With the exception of North Carolina, each of those states has lower taxes than Ohio:

Ohio

- Top personal income tax rate: 5.93 percent
- State-local tax burden: 9.7 percent
- Taxes paid per capita: $3,563
- Rank: 20

Florida

- Top personal income tax rate: 0 percent
- State-local tax burden: 9.3 percent
- Taxes paid per capita: $3,728
- Rank: 27

North Carolina

- Top personal income tax rate: 7.75 percent
- State-local tax burden: 9.9 percent
- Taxes paid per capita: $3,535
- Rank: 17

Texas

- Top personal income tax rate: 0 percent
- State-local tax burden: 7.9 percent
- Taxes paid per capita: $3,104
- Rank: 45

South Carolina

- Top personal income tax rate: 7 percent
- State-local tax burden: 8.4 percent
- Taxes paid per capita: $2,760
- Rank: 41

Arizona

- Top personal income tax rate: 4.54 percent
- State-local tax burden: 8.4 percent
- Taxes paid per capita: $3,006
- Rank: 40

So, the Buckeye State took a bit of a beating when it came to the movement of AGI. Let's look at its biggest MSA, Cleveland.

Like many midwestern cities, Cleveland's history is one of commerce and manufacturing, and it was once the country's fifth largest city, behind New York, Boston, Philadelphia, and Chicago. Its location on Lake Erie has long made it a prime hub for shipping and transportation.

But like many midwestern cities, Cleveland fell on hard times in the 1970s and early 1980s. Investment and redevelopment, especially along the waterfront and downtown areas, gave the city a much-needed boost in recent years. New sports arenas and complexes were built and the city became home to the Rock and Roll Hall of Fame.

Nevertheless, the metropolitan area continued to suffer, losing $5.2 billion in AGI between 1995 and 2010, almost three times the combined $1.7 billion value of the Cleveland Browns, Cavaliers, and Indians.[8]

The Cleveland MSA—officially known as Cleveland-Elyria-Mentor, OH—has a population of just over two million people, down 25,000 from 1990, according to the Census Bureau. The Cleveland MSA covers 3,756 square miles in these Ohio counties:

- Cuyahoga County
- Geauga County
- Lake County
- Lorain County
- Medina County

And lost $5.3 billion in AGI to:

1.	Summit County, OH (Akron MSA)	$670 million
2.	Portage County, OH (Akron MSA)	$250 million
3.	Maricopa County, AZ (Phoenix MSA)	$220 million
4.	Lee County, FL (Cape Coral MSA)	$220 million
5.	Collier County, FL (Naples MSA)	$170 million
6.	Palm Beach County, FL (Miami MSA)	$150 million
7.	Franklin County, OH (Columbus MSA)	$130 million
8.	Clark County, NV (Las Vegas MSA)	$130 million
9.	Mecklenberg, SC (Charlotte MSA)	$110 million
10.	Sarasota County, FL (North Port MSA)	$100 million

Again, we see a similar pattern with the other midwestern MSAs: some of the migrating income stayed close by, but much of it went to—yes—areas with lower taxes, like Arizona, Florida, Nevada, and South Carolina.

Taxes may not be the only reason people move, but over and over again we see the same thing: working wealth leaving high-tax areas for the comforts of lower-tax environs. The numbers say it all.

There is one area of the country that we haven't covered, and it happens to round out the top 10 list of the states and MSAs that saw the greatest net gains in AGI from 1995 to 2010—the South, specifically Georgia and the Atlanta MSA and Texas and the Austin MSA. Let's look at them next.

Scan here for supplemental and additional material, illustrations, video, and other information.

Chapter Nine Endnotes:

[1] Caterpillar and John Deere market values as of October 2012, Forbes.com.

[2] South Dakota FY2013 budget, http://www.argusleader.com/assets/pdf/DF182577126.PDF.

[3] Oprah Winfrey's net worth as of September 2012, Forbes.com,

http://www.forbes.com/profile/oprah-winfrey/.

[4] Team market valuations from Forbes.com: "The Business of Football," http://www.forbes.com/nfl-valuations/list/, and "The Business of Basketball," http://www.forbes.com/nba-valuations/list/.

[5] Kellogg's 2011 revenue, Forbes.com.

[6] NFL and NBA team valuations, see note four. MBA team valuation, "The Business of Baseball," http://www.forbes.com/mlb-valuations/list/, and NHL team valuation, "The Business of Hockey," http://www.forbes.com/nhl-valuations/list/.

[7] Molly Bloom, "Ohio State University Has the 31st Largest Endowment in the Nation, Stateimpact.com (February 1, 2012), http://stateimpact.npr.org/ohio/2012/02/01/ohio-state-university-has-the-31st-largest-endowment-in-the-nation/.

[8] See notes four and six.

Chapter Ten

A Personal Perspective

I KNOW WHY MONEY WALKS

By Victor Sperandeo

When the United States of America was formed, individual states were created with specific rights and powers to determine their own laws and policies. This would allow each state to retain some autonomy and create healthy competition between them. If one state abused its residents, they would be free to pack their bags and move to another state to enjoy a better situation.

Of course, one of the primary issues that greatly affects the decision-making process of Americans is taxes. The states that have high income tax-

es face the problem of keeping people who are truly rich from domiciling themselves in a more tax-friendly state.

Why would someone leave his home state for another? Let's use a few assumptions to answer that question:

1. Municipal bond interest yields 5 percent.
2. The person earns $1 million per year.
3. The person has a high savings rate and does not spend every penny he or she earns.

What is really the quantity of cash we are talking about over a 10-year period?

If someone lives in New York City and earns $1 million, the taxes paid to the state and city is a combined 12.63 percent. So, for simplicity, after a maximum federal tax rate and deduction after 2012 (assuming the state tax deduction is maintained), on a million dollars a net tax of $76,000 is paid to New York. If the individual lived in a state with no state income tax (such as Texas or Florida), they could then save the $76,000 per year. Invested in municipal bonds for 10 years at 5 percent interest, the total amount in the investor's pocket is an extra *$1,003,716,* or more than

a full year's earnings. Under this scenario, just by living in a different state, one with no income tax, someone could save an entire year's income over a 10-year working period. This is certainly not a small amount of money.

Taxes matter quite a bit, contrary to what Warren Buffet claims about higher taxes on investing not affecting investment. For example, if a long-term investor invested $100 in the S&P 500 after President Nixon went off the gold standard in 1971, they would have a total of $4,764.45 at the end of 2011. When you deduct the original investment of $100 he would have earned a compounded annual return of 9.95 percent.

At first blush, anyone would be happy with a return of nearly 10 percent. However, after inflation of 4.38 percent (and the official Bureau of Labor Statistic's consumer price index numbers are very understated in my opinion), the real return is $750.22, not the pre-inflation $4,764.45. Sell the investment, pay the current 15 percent long-term capital gains tax rate on the profit (which is a tax of $714.67), and your after-inflation gain is now only $35.55, assuming no state taxes on your gain.

This lowers the return to 0.74 basis points per year (about ¾ of 1 percent annually) over 41 years! Imagine if the New York State and New York City taxes of 12.63 percent were also paid? And if President Obama's tax rates existed (23.8 percent)? The net loss would be $381.34, which means *you are being taxed on an after-inflation loss.*

The government is clearly confiscating the people's wealth. To quote John Maynard Keynes from *The Economic Consequences of the Peace*:

> There is no subtler, no surer means of overturning the existing basis of society than to debauch the currency. The process engages all the hidden forces of economic law on the side of destruction, and does it in a manner which not one man in a million is able to diagnose.

More interesting is that Keynes took the phrase "debauch the currency" from none other than Vladimir Lenin, who stated that the best way to destroy the capitalist system was "to debauch the currency."

So to prevent the total confiscation of capital, via inflation and taxes, the key is to *not* tax capital at all. From a different point of view, this is why

the Democrats linked the consumer price index to Social Security payments in 1975 after the end of the gold standard, as they understood and planned for inflation, trying to protect themselves from the anger of a large voting bloc.

The high taxes charged by some states are the nail in the coffin of building wealth. The "rich" merely have to live in Florida or Texas for 182 days a year to avoid paying state income taxes, and this is very easy to do. Eventually the high-tax states will lose their investor base and turn into an economic Greece.

Although you can deny reality, you can't deny its consequences.

Victor Sperandeo is the president and CEO of Alpha Financial Technologies. He has been a professional trader, index developer, and financial market commentator for over 45 years and has traded independently and for notable investors including George Soros and Leon Cooperman. He is also the author of Trader Vic: Methods of a Wall Street Master.

Chapter Ten

THE SOUTH RISES

Great gains in Texas and Georgia

Of the top 10 states and MSAs that gained and lost the most adjusted gross income (AGI) between 1995 and 2010, we can see a definite pattern: the states with lower personal income tax rates and lower per capita state tax burdens fared far better in terms of AGI migration than those with higher taxes. In short, working wealth appeared to move to better places, tax-wise.

We saw how the eastern part of the U.S. and its MSAs fared—not well. We saw how California fared—not well. We saw how the Midwest fared—not well. And we saw how two desert states, Arizona and Nevada, and one giant southern state, Florida, fared—extremely well.

There are two MSAs left to talk about from our top 10 list, Atlanta and Austin, both of which saw tremendous gains. Not surprisingly, their states—Texas and Georgia—also did very well in the migration of adjusted gross income and also appear in the top 10 list of states that saw the greatest net gains in AGI.

In fact, the South makes a very strong showing here. Of the 10 states that saw the greatest net gains of AGI from 1995 to 2010, six are in the south:

- Florida, which gained $86.4 billion
- Texas, which gained $22.1 billion
- North Carolina, which gained $21.6 billion
- South Carolina, which gained $13 billion
- Georgia, which gained $12.4 billion
- Tennessee, which gained $8.3 billion

Of those, Florida, Texas, and Tennessee have no state personal income tax.

We're going to round out the book by covering the remaining two MSAs that gained the most wealth between 1995 and 2010, Austin and Atlanta.

TEXAS TAKES IT IN

Texas is a great state, with great cities, great culture, and a great climate, both in terms of weather (well, depending on the season) and taxes. The state of Texas has zero personal income tax and a very low state tax burden per capita, $3,104, one of the lowest in the nation (ranking: 45th in the country).

The state of Texas gained $22.1 billion in AGI from 1995 to 2010. That is a tremendous amount of money, equivalent to about eight times the $2.7 billion net worth of Dallas Cowboys' owner Jerry Jones.[1]

TEXAS TAX FACTS	
	Top personal income tax rate: 0%
	State-local tax burden: 7.9% Taxes paid per capita: $3,104 Rank: 45
	Net gain of AGI: $22.1 billion

So, where did all that AGI come from? Here are the top five states from which AGI moved to Texas:

- California, $4.7 billion
- Louisiana, $3 billion
- Illinois, $2 billion
- New York, $1.5 billion
- Michigan, $1.2 billion

Every one of those states has a higher personal income tax rate and higher per capita state tax burden than Texas. And, of course, we can drill down to the specific, county-level movement and see exactly from which counties in which states that working wealth came to Texas between 1995 and 2010:

1.	Los Angeles County, CA (LA MSA)	$1.7 billion
2.	Orleans Parish, LA (New Orleans MSA)	$1.1 billion
3.	Orange County, CA (LA MSA)	$776 million
4.	Cook County, IL (Chicago MSA)	$703 million
5.	Jefferson Parish, LA (New Orleans MSA)	$654 million
6.	St. Louis County, MO (St. Louis MSA)	$491 million
7.	Tulsa County, OK (Tulsa MSA)	$471 million
8.	San Diego County, CA (San Diego MSA)	$450 million
9.	San Bernardino County, CA (Riverside MSA)	$401 million
10.	East Baton Rouge Parish, LA (Baton Rouge MSA)	$357 million

As we have seen in other states that gained AGI, much of it comes from familiar sources: California and Illinois, where taxes are appreciably higher. And big chunks came from St. Louis, New Orleans, and Baton Rouge, too, all of which are MSAs in states with high taxes, poor economic performances, or both:

- Missouri ranks 38th in economic performance on the 2012 ALEC-Laffer State Economic Performance Index and seventh in economic outlook.
- Louisiana, which was slammed by two hurricanes in five years, ranks 25th in economic performance and 19th in economic outlook.
- Like California and Illinois, both Missouri and Louisiana have higher personal income tax rates and state per capita tax burdens than Texas.
- Texas ranks second in the country in economic performance on the ALEC-Laffer Index and has an economic outlook ranking of 16.

So, Texas saw a net gain of $22.1 billion in AGI. That's the combined value of all of Texas's professional sports teams—the Texas Rangers, Houston Astros, Dallas Cowboys, Houston Texans, Dallas Mavericks, San Antonio

Spurs, and Houston Rockets.[2] Let's look at two of its MSAs, Austin and Dallas, which, together, gained $14.5 billion in AGI. (Dallas isn't in the top 10, but because it gained so much and is in Texas, we include it here.)

AUSTIN ROCKS

Austin, the capital of Texas, is one of the most vibrant cities in America, much loved for its nightlife, restaurants, live music, and dynamic cultural scene. Austin is the home of the wildly popular and influential South by Southwest Festival, which epitomizes the spirit of Austin by combining music, film, culture, and technology in one event. SXSW, as it is called, is somewhat of a movement and shows how important Austin has become in the worlds of business and culture.

Home to the University of Texas, Austin is also famed for its entrepreneurial spirit and has emerged as an incubator for emerging technologies and ideas—it's Texas's own Silicon Valley. Austin is also beautiful. It sits on the Colorado River and is surrounded by three man-made lakes. Though the summers are hot and humid, the winters are mild and dry. Austin averages 300 days of sunshine a year and an average temperature of 68 degrees.

No wonder it has grown so much. According to the Census Bureau, Austin has a population of 820,611, up 20 percent from 2000 and up nearly 50 percent from 1990, making it one of the fastest growing cities in the U.S.

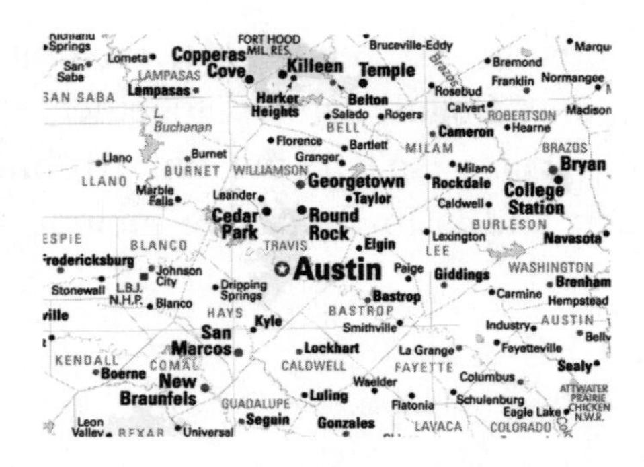

The Austin MSA, which is officially the Austin-Round Rock-San Marcos MSA, grew even more. The current population of the Austin MSA is 1.7 million, up nearly 30 percent from 2000 and up 50 percent from 1990. More than 870,000 people moved to Austin between 1990 and 2010, 500,000 in the last 10 years alone. It's a boomtown.

And it also saw an influx of $8 billion in AGI between 1995 and 2010, the 10th largest gain of any MSA in the country over the same period. That's about eight times the current lifetime box office gross of Texas native and former Austin resident Mathew McConaughey.[3]

Let's look closer at the Austin MSA. The MSA covers 4,279 square miles and these five counties:

- Bastrop County
- Caldwell County
- Hays County
- Travis County
- Williamson County

And here's where that $8 billion came from:

1.	Harris County, TX (Houston MSA)	$950 million
2.	Dallas County, TX (Dallas MSA)	$420 million
3.	Los Angeles County, CA (LA MSA)	$290 million
4.	Santa Clara County, CA (San Jose MSA)	$270 million
5.	Bexar County, TX (San Antonio MSA)	$220 million
6.	Bell County, TX (Killeen-Fort Hood MSA)	$170 million
7.	Collin County, TX (Dallas MSA)	$160 million
8.	Tarrant County, TX (Dallas MSA)	$150 million
9.	Orange County, CA (LA MSA)	$140 million
10.	Cook County, IL (Chicago MSA)	$140 million

As we can see, a lot of AGI came to Austin from other parts of Texas. But much of it also came from the usual suspects: California and Illinois.

Austin is a great place to live, so there is little wonder why people would move there. Let's look at another Texas MSA to gain AGI, Dallas-Ft. Worth.

DALLAS DOES WELL

Dallas will be forever synonymous with three things: oil money, J.R. Ewing, and the Dallas Cowboys. But Dallas, along with its neighbors and partner cities, Ft. Worth and Arlington, is a major player in corporate America. Dozens of giant firms are headquartered or have offices there, including American Airlines, Dell, HP, Lockheed Martin, Texas Instruments, and ExxonMobil, the world's largest company, according to Forbes.

It's a powerful area, and a large one, too. According to the Census Bureau, the population of Dallas is 1.2 million; Ft. Worth, 758,000; and Arlington, 374,000. But the Dallas metropolitan statistical area is much, much larger—6.4 million people, the fourth largest in the country.

The Dallas MSA—officially the Dallas-Ft. Worth-Arlington MSA—covers a lot of ground, 9,286 square miles over these 12 counties:

- Collin County
- Dallas County
- Delta County
- Denton County
- Ellis County
- Hunt County
- Johnson County
- Kaufman County
- Parker County
- Rockwall County
- Tarrant County
- Wise County

And the Dallas MSA gained $6.5 billion (about 5.4 times the $1.2 billion net worth of Dallas's great oilman, T. Boone Pickens)[4]. That's the 12th biggest gain of any MSA in the country over this period of time.

Here are the top 10 places that AGI came from:

1. Los Angeles County, CA (LA MSA) $590 million
2. Orange County, CA (LA MSA) $350 million
3. Lubbock County, TX (Lubbock MSA) $310 million
4. Orleans Parish, LA (New Orleans MSA) $280 million
5. Harris County, TX (Houston MSA) $280 million
6. St. Louis County, MO (St. Louis MSA) $260 million
7. Tulsa County, OK (Tulsa MSA) $250 million
8. El Paso County, TX (El Paso MSA) $250 million
9. Oklahoma County, OK (Oklahoma City MSA) $250 million
10. Cook County, IL (Chicago MSA) $240 million

So, as with Austin, we see a lot of the AGI moving from within the state, but, again, a big chunk came from California and Illinois.

Now, Dallas has a lot going for it, but are people moving there for the culture? The weather? The football? No judgment here, but what Dallas has going for it, above all else, is a great state tax regime: zero percent state personal income tax and one of the lowest per capita state tax burdens in the country (45th), just $3,104 per person. The ALEC-Laffer index gives Texas high marks, too, ranking it second in the nation in terms of economic performance and 16th in economic outlook. Things look good for the Lone Star State.

But Texas is not alone in great gains of working wealth. Let's head over to Georgia, another southern state that saw big increases in AGI.

GEORGIA'S JUST PEACHY

Like Texas, Georgia did just peachy when it came to the migration of working wealth. Between 1995 and 2010, Georgia saw a net gain of $12.4 billion in AGI, the seventh highest gain in the country. That gain of $12.4 billion is about twice the market value of Georgia-based Newell Rubbermaid, the maker of Sharpies and other iconic office supplies.[5]

GEORGIA TAX FACTS
Top personal income tax rate: 6%
State-local tax burden: 9% Taxes paid per capita: $3,222 Rank: 33
Net gain of AGI: $12.4 billion

Here are the top 10 states that the $12.4 billion came from:

1.	New York	$2 billion
2.	New Jersey	$1.1 billion
3.	Illinois	$870 million
4.	Ohio	$810 million
5.	Michigan	$779 million
6.	California	$647 million
7.	Pennsylvania	$590 million
8.	Connecticut	$372 million
9.	Maryland	$366 million
10.	Massachusetts	$357 million

And, as always, we can drill down even more specifically. Here are the top 10 counties from which that $12.4 billion in AGI came from:

1. Broward County, FL (Pompano Beach MSA) $710 million
2. Cook County, IL (Chicago MSA) $481 million
3. Queens County, NY (NY MSA) $440 million
4. Los Angeles County, CA (LA MSA) $427 million
5. Kings County, NY (NY MSA) $303 million
6. Palm Beach County, FL (Miami MSA) $257 million
7. Fairfield County, CT (Bridgeport MSA) $257 million
8. Nassau County, NY (NY MSA) $255 million
9. Orleans Parish, LA (New Orleans MSA) $248 million
10. Suffolk County, NY (NY MSA) $230 million

Again, we see a lot of income moving from the same places—Illinois, New York, California—all higher tax states. Let's look at Georgia's biggest MSA, Atlanta, which also gained AGI.

ATLANTA'S ON FIRE

The Atlanta–Sandy Springs–Marietta MSA is the ninth largest in the nation, with 5.3 million people. Like the Austin MSA, Atlanta grew like kudzu. In 1990, the population was 3.1 million. In 2000, the population was 4.2 million. Ten years later, in 2010, the population was 5.3 million. The Atlanta MSA grew by more than a million people in just 10 years. Stunning. Metaphorically, of course, Atlanta's on fire.

As MSAs go, Atlanta is one of the largest in terms of area, covering 8,376 square miles and a whopping 28 counties:

- Barrow County
- Bartow County
- Butts County
- Carroll County
- Cherokee County
- Clayton County
- Cobb County
- Coweta County
- Dawson County
- DeKalb County
- Douglas County
- Fayette County
- Forsyth County
- Fulton County
- Gwinnett County
- Haralson County
- Heard County
- Henry County
- Jasper County
- Lamar County
- Meriwether County
- Newton County
- Paulding County

- Pickens County
- Pike County
- Rockdale County
- Spalding County
- Walton County

The Atlanta MSA saw a net gain of $9 billion in AGI between 1995 and 2010. That's four-and-a-half times Ted Turner's net worth.[6] And here is the top 10 list of where it came from:

1. Broward County, FL (Pompano Beach MSA) $600 million
2. Queens County, NY (NYC MSA) $420 million
3. Cook County, IL (Chicago MSA) $410 million
4. Los Angeles County, CA (LA MSA) $370 million
5. Kings County, NY (NYC MSA) $280 million
6. Nassau County, NY (NYC MSA) $240 million
7. Orleans Parish, LA (New Orleans MSA) $230 million
8. Suffolk County, NY (NYC MSA) $200 million
9. Fairfield County, CT (NYC MSA) $200 million
10. Oakland County, MI (Detroit MSA) $190 million

Again we see the same pattern: AGI moving from around the region, but also from states with much higher tax rates, like New York, Illinois, California, Connecticut, and Michigan.

Atlanta is one of the fastest growing cities in America. The city and state are home to some of the country's largest and most recognizable corporations, including Aflac, Arby's, Coca-Cola, Delta, Home Depot, UPS, and Wendy's. And both the state and the Atlanta MSA have see billions in AGI move there. Is it because of Georgia's relatively low tax structure?

Georgia

- Top income tax rate: 6 percent
- State-local tax burden: 9 percent
- Taxes paid per capita: $3,222
- Rank: 33

Maybe. Whatever the reason, the state saw $12.4 billion in AGI move there from 1995 to 2010. It's extraordinary. Now, its ALEC-Laffer economic performance ranking isn't that great. In fact, Georgia ranked 33rd in the nation in terms of performance. But its economic outlook ranking is very high: 10th in the country. When it comes to setting economic expectations for Atlanta in the future, describing the birth town of Coca-Cola and Home Depot as the "Chicago of the South" may no longer be necessary, or even thought of as a compliment.

Scan here for supplemental and additional material, illustrations, video, and other information.

Chapter Ten Endnotes:

[1] Jerry Jones's net worth as of September 2012, $2.7 billion, http://www.forbes.com/profile/jerry-jones/.

[2] Team market values from Forbes.com: "The Business of Baseball,"

http://www.forbes.com/mlb-valuations/list/; "The Business of Football," http://www.forbes.com/nfl-valuations/list/; and "The Business of Basketball," http://www.forbes.com/nba-valuations/list/.

[3] Mathew McConaughey's lifetime box office gross as of October 2012, $1,174,950,988; http://www.boxofficemojo.com/people/chart/?id=matthewmcconaughey.htm.

[4] T. Boone Pickens net worth as of September 2012, $1.2 billion, http://www.forbes.com/profile/t-boone-pickens/.

[5] Newell Rubbermaid market value as of October 2012, Forbes.com.

[6] Ted Turner's net worth as of September 2012, $2 billion, http://www.forbes.com/profile/ted-turner/.

Conclusion

THE PATH TO PROSPERITY

Welcome wealth—and growth—by offering incentives and opportunity

Incentives within tax codes matter. Taxes may not be the sole reason Americans moved $2 trillion of their AGI between the states, but there is a clear and unmistakable pattern here: incomes moved to where taxes were lower. Tax policy can be a tremendous incentive, and the mode of taxation matters the most. Some states—like Florida and Texas—got it right, while some states—like California and New York—got it wrong (and continue to get it wrong).

America is, and always has been, a great working laboratory of democracy. Each state serves as a model for what works and what doesn't work, for what *is* working and for what is *not* working. Look no further than to the states. And then look at how people behave. People vote by ballot, but they also vote with their feet. And what we might be seeing with this extraordinary movement of working wealth is a repudiation of what is *not* working for millions of Americans—high taxes. By moving, they are voting for what they want—lower tax regimes.

The evidence is compelling: Between 1995 and 2010, the nine states that have no personal state income taxes enjoyed massive net influxes of AGI (over $146 billion). The states with the highest personal income tax rates saw massive losses ($107.2 billion). The states with the lowest overall per capita tax burdens saw great gains in AGI ($69.9 billion), while the states with the highest per capita tax burdens saw stunning losses ($139 billion).

The nine states with *no* personal income taxes	**GAINED $146 BILLION**
The nine states with the *highest* personal income taxes	**LOST $107.2 BILLION**
The 10 states with the *lowest* per capita state tax burdens	**GAINED $69.9 BILLION**
The 10 states with the *highest* per capita state tax burden	**LOST $139 BILLION**

Taxes matter. *A lot.* And the tax that matters the most? Personal income tax. Is this definitive proof that taxes, either state personal income or overall tax burden, are the number one reason money migrates? No. Is it compelling? Absolutely. Just look at the numbers and the mapping. It's undeniable. And there is other evidence, too.

According to *Rich States, Poor States,* published by the American Legislative Exchange Council (ALEC), the nine states with no personal income taxes saw their populations grow by an average of 13.7 percent, about 148 percent higher than the average of high-tax states and 58 percent higher than the American average.[1] Why is this important? Because, according to ALEC, population increases in those states resulted in stronger economies, larger tax bases, and an overall increase in tax revenue, despite having zero income taxes.

Furthermore, between 2001 and 2010, those nine states with no income tax dramatically outperformed the nine states with the highest income taxes in three major categories: population, state product, and employment. When the authors of the study compared all 50 states and the District of Columbia, they found that "the no income tax states outperformed their high tax counterparts across the board in gross state product growth, population growth, job growth, and, perhaps shockingly, even tax receipt growth."[2]

Real economic expansion—which includes the attraction of people and their working wealth—does not happen when tax regimes are unfriendly to income and investment. This is evidenced by the migration of wealth, which we have just documented, and by the findings of studies like *Rich States, Poor States*. That study shows that states that tax personal income decline as a share of U.S. GDP, while states that do not tax personal income have growing GDPs. ALEC reports that the nine no-income-tax states today are outperforming the other 41 states, so we have strong evidence of what works. As the authors of *Rich States* put it: "If we had to summarize the findings of this publication and our comparative analysis of state policy in one sentence, it would be this: Be more like Texas and less like California."[3]

TEXAS	CALIFORNIA
Gained $22.1 billion	Lost $31.8 billion
Top personal income tax rate: 0%	Top marginal personal income tax rate: 13.3%
State-local tax burden: 7.9% (sixth lowest in the country)	State-local tax burden: 11.2% (fourth highest in the country)

Taxes aren't the only factor in growth and movement of wealth, of course, and many organizations, like the Tax Foundation, are quick to point that out. People move for all sorts of reasons. But taxes can be a profound incentive, as the *Wall Street Journal* editorialized last February:

> The tax burden isn't the only factor that determines investment flows and growth. But it is a major signal about how a state treats business, investment, and risk-taking. States like New York, California, Illinois, and Maryland that have high and rising tax rates also tend to be those that have growing welfare states, heavy regulation, dominant public unions, and budgets that are subject to boom and bust because they rely so heavily on a relatively few rich taxpayers.[4]

And those taxpayers—rich and middle class alike—are leaving in droves, as we have just seen.

~

Of course, some states and MSAs have natural advantages that others do not. Some places must work harder than others to attract businesses, investments, and people. For example, all things being equal, where would you rather spend your winter? Miami or Detroit? Phoenix or Cleveland? LA or Boston? Let's face it. Few people probably migrate to Nevada for the scenery, so having a pro-growth, incentivized tax code is part of attracting people and working wealth. And as we have seen in the data, it seems to be working.

No matter what natural charms your state possesses, if you want more revenue, you have to have a pro-growth tax policy. And a pro-growth tax policy means low taxes. It's that simple. You want to attract working wealth? You want to attract corporations? You want to attract people? Your tax policies must be pro-growth. And that means that state taxes, particularly personal income taxes, must be low. The lower (or non-existent) they are, the more growth.

Governments must and absolutely should collect taxes, but it is the mode of taxation that matters most. The more mobile we are the less able governments will be to collect taxes on income. So the best way to generate revenue is not to tax a mobile resource like income, but to tax consumption, sales on consumer goods, property, etc. You want to collect revenue in the most benign way possible, and the best way to do that is not to tax an increasingly mobile resource (i.e. income), but to tax those things that are legitimately still fixed on consumption: again, sales and use taxes, property taxes, etc.

Higher government revenue does not come from higher taxes. The opposite is true: the lower the taxes, the broader the tax base and the greater the revenues. The *Wall Street Journal*, in the same editorial quoted above, noted that states with no income taxes "have also recorded faster revenue growth to pay for government services over the past two decades than states with income taxes. That's because growth in the economy from attracting jobs and capital has meant greater tax collections."

We see this over and over again. Lower taxes attract more people, which in turn creates a broader tax base, which in turn results in economic growth and higher tax revenues across the board.

California is a terrific example of this. A vibrant, attractive state, California leads the way in many fields. And certain counties and areas in California still show evidence of growth (the Riverside MSA for example). But California also leads the way in high state taxes. California has the highest personal income tax rates in the nation and the fourth highest per capita taxes in the country. And we see what has happened: from 1995 to 2010, the state of California lost $31.8 billion in AGI. And California lost it to states with overwhelmingly lower tax environments–Nevada, Arizona, Oregon, Texas, and Washington, three of which have no personal income taxes and all of which have markedly lower per capita taxes.

The number one place Californians migrated with their AGI? Clark County, Nevada, with a personal income tax of zero and a state-local per capita tax burden of just $3,297, one of the lowest in the country. The amount people can save by moving just a few hundred miles from a high-tax state like California to a low-tax state like Nevada is tremendous. It can be the difference between being able to own a home, put a kid through college, or invest in your retirement. And the choice is yours.

But what if you can't move? What if you can't vote with your feet? What can you do? You can encourage your elected officials to pay attention to this issue and make decisions that are more pro-growth. And your politicians can take tax policy more seriously, by looking at the facts.

And what if declining states take no action? From the data we mapped, we can draw some conclusions. In this case, I think past performance will be an indicator of future behavior. If they do not take action, or take the wrong action (like continue to raise personal income taxes), states that already experienced losses will continue to see a drain of both people and AGI. More and more people will continue to move, leaving the rest of the citizens holding the bag.

Why? Because governments react in irrational ways. If they were rational, they would have seen these numbers and acted to either curb the outflow or encourage an inflow. But most governments, like most people, do not behave rationally, which is why states like California, when faced with mounting deficits, raise taxes. That, in turn, drives people, income, and investments away. And that, in turn, leaves the remaining taxpayers to shoulder an ever-increasing burden.

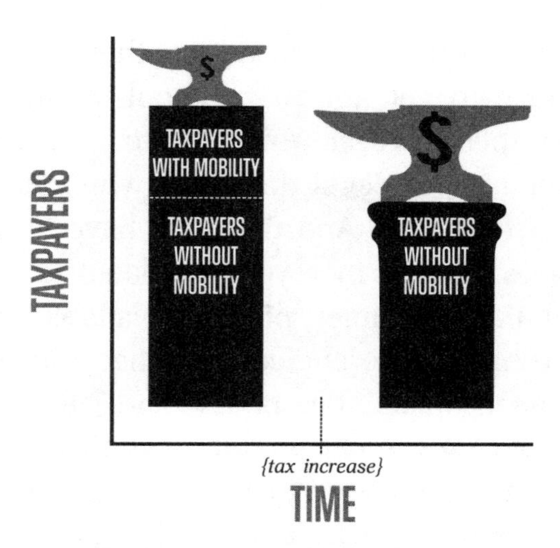

And with a smaller economic pulse, the economic challenges are compounded, making growth and development more difficult. In short, if states do nothing to stem the tide of their massive income losses, here is what you can expect:

- More movement of working wealth to pro-growth places
- Higher costs to those who remain
- An economic death spiral in terms of growth and development

Based on the evidence provided in previous chapters, if your state and local tax code is based on something outdated—like heavily taxing a mobile resource like personal income—your state will continue to fail to collect adequate revenues and continue to decline. The extremes will apply faster, as more and more people will make the choice to move, which will put more strain on state economies and governments. If you are losing working wealth and take no action to stop it, your challenges will only get worse.

And if you are a politician in one of those states you are going to have to get honest and look at the facts. You can't ignore them forever. You need to explain why your state has the tax policies it does, and why your state continues down that road. And then you have to make some tough choices. The further your outdated tax codes drift away from the consumer powers available from smart devices, the harder the choices may become. You cannot have an anachronistic tax policy and be successful in the mobile age. You must provide incentives for working wealth to stay in or move to your state. Otherwise, your wealth will continue to walk.

~

For the states in good shape now, the ones with the pro-growth tax policies, it is mission critical to protect and preserve such advantages. If you are attracting working wealth, the gains are tremendous: a greater tax base, greater development, greater growth, etc. Those states—like Florida, Nevada, Tennessee, and Texas—that are doing all the right things should be proud of their policies, and other states should look to them for guidance and inspiration.

Political courage can be rewarded, and governors across the country are taking steps to flatten, reduce, or streamline state tax regimes. Governors are starting to act, and they are changing the trajectory of their economies. One need only look to Kansas for the kind of leadership that others may use as a model.

There's no guarantee that your city or state will thrive forever using its current advantages. And if people remain rationally ignorant of how important personal income taxes are to their personal economic growth as well as the growth of their city or state, then cities, MSAs, and states will continue to spiral downward. They may die a slow economic death. Income is mobile, and a policy based on taxing a resource that is mobile is foolhardy. The states that understand this will thrive. The states that ignore this simple fact will continue to be plagued with challenges.

Look at the data: which states and MSAs are healthy and which are sick? Which are attracting incomes and which are not? Which ones are growing and which are dying? Where is working wealth walking? What correlations can we draw?

So, if you are a winner, don't screw it up. If you are a loser, if you do not take action, the evidence of the past is a clear predictor of what the future holds: you will continue to lose working wealth. If you do not understand and then address the root causes of your income migration, you will continue to lose billions of dollars. And a smaller economic pulse means that your challenges will get increasingly harder and harder to solve.

~

With knowledge comes power, and I hope that with this new knowledge—which states are gaining billions of dollars in AGI, which states are losing billions of dollars, what their tax regimes are, and why we are rationally ignorant of these facts—we can have a rational, national discussion about tax policy.

Most people don't want to talk about taxes and tax policy, but there is no other issue that so directly affects the prosperity of our communities and the country as a whole. And in our mobile age, the mode of taxation is critically important. The evidence suggests that those states that build incentives into their tax policies (the ones that do not tax personal income) are the ones that are thriving and will continue to thrive.

If we want our cities, our states, and our country to grow and prosper we must look at the fundamentals of economic growth. Yes, there are many, many factors at play in any economy and in any plan for growth, but there is one factor that stands out again and again—the mode of taxation matters.

As a native Missourian, I have always been struck by the straight talk that comes from our own Mark Twain. In his notebook he wrote:

> Some men worship rank, some worship heroes, some worship power, some worship God, & over these ideals they dispute & cannot unite—but they all worship money.

Perhaps it is time for those with money not already walking to do more talking.

Scan here for supplemental and additional material, illustrations, video, and other information.

Conclusion Endnotes:

[1] Arthur Laffer, Stephen B. Moore, and Nathan Williams, *Rich States Poor States: ALEC-Laffer State Economic Competitiveness Index*, fifth edition (Washington, DC: American Legislative Exchange Council, October 2012), http://www.alec.org/docs/RSPS_5th_Edition.pdf.

[2] Ibid, p. vii.

[3] Ibid, p. 2.

[4] "The Heartland Tax Rebellion: More states want to repeal their income taxes," Review & Outlook, the *Wall Street Journal* (February 8, 2012), http://online.wsj.com/article/SB1000142405297020388990457720087215911349 2.html.

ADDENDUM

A. THE 10 STATES WITH THE GREATEST NET GAINS OF AGI, 1995-2010:

1. Florida

- Net gain: $86.4 billion
- Top income tax rate: 0 percent
- State-local tax burden: 9.3 percent
- Taxes per capita: $3,728
- National tax burden rank: 27

2. Arizona

- Net gain: $24.5 billion
- Top income tax rate: 4.54 percent
- State-local tax burden: 8.4 percent
- Taxes per capita: $3,006
- National tax burden rank: 40

3. Texas

- Net gain: $22.1 billion
- Top state income tax rate: 0 percent
- State-local tax burden: 7.9 percent
- Taxes per capita: $3,104
- National tax burden rank: 45

4. North Carolina

- Net gain: $21.6 billion
- Top income tax rate: 7.75 percent
- State-local tax burden: 9.9 percent
- Taxes per capita: $3,535
- National tax burden rank: 17

5. Nevada

- Net gain: $16 billion
- Top income tax rate: 0 percent
- State-local tax burden: 8.2 percent
- Taxes per capita: $3,297
- National tax burden rank: 42

6. South Carolina

- Net gain: $13 billion
- Top income tax rate: 7 percent
- State-local tax burden: 8.4 percent
- Per capita state tax burden $2,760
- National tax burden rank: 41

7. Georgia

- Net gain: $12.4 billion
- Top income tax rate: 6 percent
- State-local tax burden: 9 percent
- Taxes per capita: $3,222
- National tax burden rank: 33

8. Colorado

- Net gain: $11 billion
- Top income tax rate: 4.63 percent
- State-local tax burden: 9.1 percent

- Taxes per capita: $4,104
- National tax burden rank: 32

9. Washington

- Net gain: $9.9 billion
- Top income tax rate: 0 percent
- State-local tax burden: 9.3 percent
- Taxes per capita: $4,261
- National tax burden rank: 28

10. Tennessee

- Net gain: $8.3 billion
- Top income tax rate: 0 percent
- State-local tax burden: 7.7 percent
- Taxes per capita: $2,707
- National tax burden rank: 48

Total gain top 10: *$2.25 trillion*

B. THE 10 STATES THAT SAW THE GREATEST NET LOSSES OF AGI, 1995-2010:

1. New York

- Net loss: $58.6 billion
- Top income tax rate: 8.82 percent
- State-local tax burden: 12.8 percent
- Taxes per capita: $6,375
- National tax burden rank: 1 (highest in the nation)

2. California

- Net loss: $31.8 billion
- Top income tax rate: 13.3 percent

- State-local tax burden: 11.2 percent
- Taxes per capita: $4,934
- National tax burden rank: 4

3. Illinois

- Net loss: $26.1 billion
- Top income tax rate: 5 percent
- State-local tax burden: 10.2 percent
- Taxes per capita: $4,512
- National tax burden rank: 11

4. New Jersey

- Net loss: $18.5 billion
- Top income tax rate: 8.97 percent
- State-local tax burden: 12.4 percent
- Taxes per capita: $6,689
- National tax burden rank: 2

5. Ohio

- Net loss: $17.1 billion
- Top income tax rate: 5.93 percent
- State-local tax burden: 9.7 percent
- Taxes per capita: $3,563
- National tax burden rank: 20

6. Michigan

- Net loss: $15.6 billion
- Top income tax rate: 4.35 percent
- State-local tax burden: 9.8 percent
- Taxes per capita: $3,503
- National tax burden rank: 18

7. Massachusetts

- Net loss: $10.8 billion
- Top income tax rate: 5.3 percent
- State-local tax burden: 10.4 percent
- Taxes per capita: $5,422
- National tax burden rank: 8

8. Pennsylvania

- Net loss: $6.9 billion
- Top income tax rate: 3.07 percent
- State-local tax burden: 10.2 percent
- Taxes per capita: $4,183
- National tax burden rank: 10

9. Maryland

- Net loss: $6.5 billion
- Top income tax rate: 5.5 percent
- State-local tax burden: 10.2 percent
- Taxes per capita: $5,234
- National tax burden rank: 12

10. Connecticut

- Net loss: $6.1 billion
- Top income tax rate: 6.7 percent
- State-local tax burden: 12.3 percent
- Taxes per capita: $6,984
- National tax burden rank: 3

Total loss bottom 10: *$198 billion*

Sources for A and B: IRS, Statistics of Income Division. Tax rates and rankings from the Tax Foundation, "Annual State-Local Tax Burden Ranking," October 2012.

C. THE 10 MSAS THAT GAINED THE MOST AGI, 1995-2010:

RANK	MSA	NET GAIN
1	Phoenix-Mesa-Scottsdale, AZ	$17.1 billion
2	Miami-Ft.Lauderdale-Miami Beach, FL	$11.9 billion
3	Las Vegas-Paradise, NV	$11.6 billion
4	Riverside-San Bernardino-Ontario, CA	$11.1 billion
5	Naples-Marco Island, FL	$10.1 billion
6	Tampa-St. Petersburg-Clearwater, FL	$9.2 billion
7	Cape Coral-Fort Myers, FL	$9 billion
8	Atlanta-Sandy Springs-Marietta, GA	$9 billion
9	Sarasota-Bradenton-Venice, FL	$8.8 billion
10	Austin-Round Rock, TX	$8 billion

D. THE 10 MSAS THAT LOST THE MOST AGI, 1995-2010:

RANK	MSA	NET LOSS
1	New York-Northern New Jersey-Long Island, NY-NJ-PA	$66.1 billion
2	Los Angeles-Long Beach-Santa Ana, CA	$31.5 billion
3	Chicago-Naperville-Joliet, IL-IN-WI	$21.1 billion
4	Detroit-Warren-Livonia, MI	$12.5 billion
5	San Jose-Sunnyvale-Santa Clara, CA	$12.3 billion
6	Washington-Arlington-Alexandria, DC-VA-MD-WV	$11.3 billion
7	Boston-Cambridge-Quincy, MA-NH	$10.3 billion
8	San Francisco-Oakland-Fremont, CA	$10.2 billion
9	Philadelphia-Camden-Wilmington, PA-NJ-DE-MD	$6.3 billion
10	Cleveland-Elyria-Mentor, OH	$5.23 billion

Source for C and D: Internal Revenue Service, Statistics of Income Division.

E. THE NINE STATES WITH ZERO STATE PERSONAL INCOME TAX:

STATE	NET GAIN (OR LOSS)
Alaska	($1.4 billion)
Florida	$86.4 billion
New Hampshire	$3.2 billion
Nevada	$16 billion
South Dakota	$528 million
Tennessee	$8.3 billion
Texas	$22 billion
Washington	$9.9 billion
Wyoming	$1.3 billion

Total gained: *$146.2 billion*

F. THE NINE STATES WITH THE HIGHEST PERSONAL INCOME TAX RATES:

RANK	STATE	NET GAIN (OR LOSS)
1	California (13.3%)	($31.8 billion)
2	Hawaii (11%)	$198 million
3	Oregon (9.9%)	$5.6 billion
4	Iowa (8.98%)	($3.2 billion)
5	New Jersey (8.97%)	($18.5 billion)
6	Vermont (8.95%)	$693 million
7	Washington, DC (8.9%)	($3.4 billion)
8	New York (8.82%)	($58.6 billion)
9	Maine (8.5%)	$1.6 billion

Total lost: *$107.4 billion*

Source for E and F: Internal Revenue Service, Statistics of Income Division.

G. THE 10 STATES WITH THE LOWEST STATE-LOCAL TAX BURDENS:

RANK	STATE	NET GAIN (OR LOSS)
1	Alaska	($1.4 billion)
2	South Dakota	$528 million
3	Tennessee	$8.3 billion
4	Louisiana	($6.1 billion)
5	Wyoming	$1.3 billion
6	Texas	$22.1 billion
7	New Hampshire	$3.2 billion
8	Alabama	$13 billion
9	Nevada	$16 billion
10	South Carolina	$13 billion

Total gain all 10: *$69.9 billion*

H. THE 10 STATES WITH THE HIGHEST STATE-LOCAL TAX BURDENS:

RANK	STATE	NET GAIN (OR LOSS)
1	New York	($58.6 billion)
2	New Jersey	($18.5 billion)
3	Connecticut	($6.1 billion)
4	California	($31.8 billion)
5	Wisconsin	($2.5 billion)
6	Rhode Island	($1.2 billion)
7	Minnesota	($4.1 billion)
8	Massachusetts	($10.8 billion)
9	Maine	$1.6 billion
10	Pennsylvania	($7 billion)

Total loss all 10: *$139 billion*

Sources for G and H: Tax rates from the Tax Foundation, "Annual State-Local Tax Burden Ranking," October 2012; AGI figures from the Internal Revenue Service, Statistics of Income Division, 1995 to 2010.

HOW MONEY WALKS: MEDIA APPEARANCES AND PRESENTATIONS

Travis H. Brown is available for media interviews and appearances as well as presentations to organizations, delegations, and advocacy groups. With our sophisticated data mapping and cutting-edge technology, we are able to offer visually arresting, high-impact appearances and presentations in several formats:

- An overview of the general facts and findings in *How Money Walks*
- Customized presentations specific to your state, metropolitan area, county, city, or region

Using powerful graphics and user-friendly data mapping, the presentations are engaging, informative, and eye-opening. Travis H. Brown is a great guest and a compelling speaker. To inquire about a presentation or media appearance, please contact:

Travis H. Brown
travis@howmoneywalks.com
(314) 435-4527
twitter.com/howmoneywalks
www.howmoneywalks.com

ABOUT THE AUTHOR

Travis H. Brown is a Missouri-based entrepreneur with a passion for helping cities and states grow via smart tax policies. He's a frequent contributor to Forbes.com and has appeared on various radio and television broadcasts such as Fox Business Network, Newsmax.com, the American Entrepreneur, and C-SPAN. As a state lobbyist who has advocated across 25 states over the last 20 years, his unique experience led his firm, Pelopidas, LLC (pronounced pe-LOP' a dus), to find a way to share how working wealth was moving nationwide.

Tackling tough issues that often miss their moment is a source of pride in Brown's issue-based work. Civic leaders such as the late Lamar Hunt, then the owner of the Kansas City Chiefs, hired his firm to pursue funding solutions for restoring Arrowhead Stadium in Kansas City. Medical doctors across the fields of anesthesia, cardiology, and orthopedic medicine have worked with his team to improve patient safety and tort reform laws. Over the last several years, Brown has applied his attention to increasing tax policy awareness through the passage of several statewide ballot initiatives related to earnings taxes and city governance. Brown now serves as president of Let Voters Decide, a coalition that supports state tax reform and the protection of voters' rights at the ballot box.

Brown's career advising governors, chief executives, legislators, mayors, and venture philanthropists got started by lobbying for his alma mater, the University of Missouri-Columbia. He holds undergraduate degrees in agricultural economics and political science from Mizzou, as well as an MBA from Washington University in St. Louis. His corporate work in sales, marketing, and government affairs has included such companies and clients as the American Home Products Corporation, the Monsanto Company, the Oracle Corporation, the American Petroleum Institute, and Procter & Gamble.

By bush-flying America to spread the results about where our growth is going, Brown hopes to inspire new small business champions, nonprofits, and community leaders to prepare their regions for our highly mobile, fiberhood age. Brown remains a serial small business owner at heart with his wife and Pelopidas co-owner Rachel Keller Brown, but applies his passions for flying, bird hunting, sports, and wine collecting every chance he gets.

Get engaged by following @HowMoneyWalks on Twitter, or downloading his apps at www.howmoneywalks.com.

PELOPIDAS, LLC

YOUR FREEDOM. YOUR BRAND. OUR MISSION.®

Pelopidas, LLC, is a St. Louis-based public affairs and advocacy firm. Founded in 2007 by Travis H. Brown and Rachel Keller Brown, Pelopidas provides intelligent and effective advocacy and political consulting in the fields of grassroots campaigns, coalition building, media relations, and fundraising event management. Clients include non-profits, corporations, state and local governments, advocacy groups, and political organizations and campaigns.

Pelopidas's seasoned teams of lobbyists, fundraisers, technology experts, and media professionals work in tandem to advance the personal, political, and policy-related goals of their clients.

The firm was named for the ancient Greek statesman and general Pelopidas, who founded the Sacred Band of Brothers and was known for freedom fighting, philanthropy, and community service. Travis H. Brown and Rachel Keller Brown have built an extraordinary network of passionate and professional advocates, coalition partners, and support staff to fight for the ideas and goals of their clients.

For more information, please visit: www.pelopidas.com or scan this code: